What people are saying about

DELIVER US FROM ME-VILLE

"Zimmerman's book is a searching, sober, and at times very funny, analysis of the impact that the culture of narcissism, or excessive self-importance, has on the Christian mind. It even offers escape routes out of Me-Ville—ways to keep the saving knowledge that we matter so much to God, safe from the corruption of mattering too much to ourselves. So read this book and get over yourself!"
—BEN PATTERSON, CAMPUS PASTOR OF WESTMONT COLLEGE AND AUTHOR OF *WAITING, FINDING HOPE WHEN GOD SEEMS SILENT,* AND *HE HAS MADE ME GLAD*

"David Zimmerman offers a thoughtful look at what it means to live missionally. His words will help move you to a more God-centric life—the one you were created for."
—MARGARET FEINBERG, AUTHOR OF *THE ORGANIC GOD* AND NATIONAL SPEAKER

"I just finished Deliver Us from Me-Ville. *I feel like I've emerged from a brawl, with a fresh shiner to show for it. But I'm limping away happy. The tough love and artful pen discovered in these pages forced me to see the small world I've been living in—and I want out. Thankfully,* Deliver Us from Me-Ville *has shown me a way; and on the whole, the process wasn't really even all that painful. Zimmerman's funky wit fused with his well-crafted prose to deliver wise, straight words."*
—WINN COLLIER, AUTHOR OF *RESTLESS FAITH* AND *LET GOD: THE TRANSFORMING WISDOM OF FRANCOIS FENELON*

"David Zimmerman's wry and witty Deliver Us from Me-Ville *is a wonderfully insightful look into today's self-consumed society. Never preachy, but always packed with delicious allusions, footnotes, and self-deprecating asides,* Me-Ville *entertains even as it instructs. David knows his Bible. He also knows The Blues Brothers, Thomas Merton, Bob Dylan and Dietrich Bonhoeffer. What's NOT to like?*

—ROBERT DARDEN, ASSOCIATE PROFESSOR OF JOURNALISM AT BAYLOR UNIVERSITY AND AUTHOR OF MORE THAN TWO DOZEN BOOKS, INCLUDING *PEOPLE GET READY* AND THE UPCOMING *JESUS LAUGHED*

"As I engaged with this book and began to discover the masterful way that David exposes the veiled, yet heinous human pride residing in all of us, I understood why David is the humble servant of Christ that he is. I found myself laughing at his stories one moment and feeling rightly convicted the next. Deliver Us from Me-Ville *continues to whisper its message into my soul months after finishing the book. Reading this book is dangerous to our self-centered schemes and well-managed facades of spirituality."*

—MIKE KING, PRESIDENT OF YOUTHFRONT, PASTOR AT JACOB'S WELL CHURCH IN KANSAS CITY, AND AUTHOR OF *PRESENCE-CENTERED YOUTH MINISTRY*

"Dave Zimmerman offers a timely and challenging guide out of worshipping and serving the contemporary 'holy trinity' of me, myself, and I, reminding us that our purpose can only be found in the relentless pursuit of Christ and His Kingdom. Deliver Us from Me-Ville *challenges our materialistic and selfish American-Dream distortion of Christianity, while providing a road map to the place where we belong."*

—WALT MUELLER, PRESIDENT OF CENTER FOR PARENT/YOUTH UNDERSTANDING AND AUTHOR OF *ENGAGING THE SOUL OF YOUTH CULTURE*

DELIVER US FROM
ME-VILLE

DELIVER US FROM ME-VILLE

DAVID A. ZIMMERMAN

David C. Cook®
transforming lives together

DELIVER US FROM ME-VILLE
Published by David C. Cook
4050 Lee Vance View
Colorado Springs, CO 80918 U.S.A.

David C. Cook Distribution Canada
55 Woodslee Avenue, Paris, Ontario, Canada N3L 3E5

David C. Cook U.K., Kingsway Communications
Eastbourne, East Sussex BN23 6NT, England

David C. Cook and the graphic circle C logo
are registered trademarks of Cook Communications Ministries.

The Web site addresses recommended throughout this book are offered as a resource to you. These Web sites are not intended in any way to be or imply an endorsement on the part of David C. Cook, nor do we vouch for their content.

Unless otherwise noted, Scripture quotations are taken from *THE MESSAGE*. Copyright © by Eugene H. Peterson 1993, 1994, 1995, 1996, 2000, 2001, 2002. Used by permission of NavPress Publishing Group. Scripture quotations marked NLT are taken from the *Holy Bible, New Living Translation,* copyright © 1996, 2004. Used by Permission of Tyndale House Publishers, Inc., Wheaton, Illinois 60189. All rights reserved. Scripture quotations marked NIV are taken from the *Holy Bible, New International Version®. NIV®.* Copyright © 1973, 1978, 1984 International Bible Society. Used by permission of Zondervan. All rights reserved.

LCCN 2008924985
ISBN 978-1-4347-0009-4

© 2008 David A. Zimmerman

The Team: Andrea Christian, Amy Kiechlin, and Jaci Schneider
Cover Design: Tobias Design
Interior Design: The DesignWorks Group

Printed in the United States of America
First Edition 2008

1 2 3 4 5 6 7 8 9 10

033108

◆

**Everyone flatters himself and
carries a kingdom in his breast.**

—JOHN CALVIN

◆

◆

For my dad:

Hope you're pleasantly surprised

◆

CONTENTS

Introduction:

ESCAPE FROM SUPERBIA

"Don't be so sure of yourself!" Jesus spits at me across the stage. I shake off his warning and return to my self-congratulation. I am Peter— at least for this Holy Week. I'm in our church's Easter play. Several of us have taken on the roles of Jesus' followers, acting out key moments from the Gospels, then stepping out of the scene to reflect on that moment's impact on our faith. I am Peter—the rock on whom Jesus builds his church. I am no-nonsense, a straight shooter. I call 'em as I see 'em, and I see that Jesus is the Christ, the chosen one of God. I can't believe nobody else sees it.

The nature of stage drama is that years pass in moments. No sooner have I completed my confident soliloquy—of course he's the Messiah; of course I'll follow him anywhere—than I am crouched by a fire, deny- ing that I know Jesus not once, not twice, but thrice.

Peter is among the first of Jesus' contemporaries to give up his life and follow Jesus. He's one of the first to voice the suspicion that this teacher, this wonder-worker, may just be the man of God they'd all been praying for. Peter's acknowledgment that Jesus is Christ is admirable. But no sooner had he said it than he developed his own messiah complex.

"Jesus, I won't let you suffer." "Jesus, I'll always stand by you."

"Jesus, I'll die before I betray you." Peter dismisses the faithlessness of his friends even as he boldly asserts his own greatness. Jesus may be the Messiah, but Peter is the man.

Peter's self-confidence is met by one of Jesus' harshest rebukes: "Get thee behind me, Satan!" No less than Peter—the first undisputed leader of the Christian church, mind you—is accused by no less than Jesus of doing no less than the Devil's work. A few pages later we see Peter showing himself faithless, proving that he is not the man, even as Jesus proves that he is the Messiah.

Good thing I'm not like Peter. I rehearsed these two scenes over and over again for months with the same small group of people, and I don't mind telling you, they drove me a little crazy. I don't know why they couldn't handle such a simple project. Early on I was the first bass voice in the chorus with my parts committed to memory. I was the first disciple off script, with lines memorized. I was the only cast member who wasn't giving the director back talk. That guy was lucky to have me around, I can tell you.

Hey—wait a minute …

What I gradually came to understand and even accept during that Easter production was that I was guilty of the same sin as Peter: *superbia*—Latin for pride or, more precisely, an inordinate sense of self-regard. I actually like the word *superbia;* it's cute. But it was counted by ancient Christians as one of seven deadly sins that destroyed the work of grace in the life of a believer. In the case of Peter (and of myself, I'm afraid), we can see why. The cocky self-assurance that compelled Peter to one-up his fellow disciples and to tell the Son of God that he needed to rethink his theology, this smug self-satisfaction that allowed me to quietly judge my fellow performers as we acted out the good news of the gospel—both threatened to undo good work before it could even be done. If I had run that play, no one would have had any fun. If Peter had run the universe, we would have no redemption from sin, no hope of reconciliation with God.

Superbia is one of the seven deadly sins not just because it has the capacity to be calamitous, as in the case of Peter, but because it can be so common, as in the case of myself. Self-absorption is a besetting sin among all God's children, nipping at the church's heels throughout its history, and as such it must be met by the vigilance of the people of God to hold it at bay.

RUNAWAY PRIDE

Superbia is often translated as "pride." Pride is a heightened sense of self-satisfaction; our pride comes through our accomplishments and our associations. The things we have done or said or avoided, the people, places, and things we surround ourselves with, strike us as uncommonly impressive. A friend once heard the crowd at a Duke University basketball game yell, "Our SATs are better than your SATs!" Your team may be proud of how it handles the ball, but in the minds of those fans, odds are you're dumber than Duke.

Pride is rooted in circumstance. In fact, pride is occasionally appropriate: The first in a family to earn a college degree should be proud of the accomplishment, and if he or she isn't, the rest of the family will be. Singer James Brown shouted, "Say it loud, I'm black and I'm proud," to assert the inherent worth and the cultural accomplishments of an entire race that had been otherwise persecuted and belittled in the larger society. The apostle Paul, of all people, sanctifies a kind of pride when he thanks God that he speaks in tongues, of all things, more than every-one in the Corinthian church.

But superbia is more insidious than mere pride. It's not rooted in accomplishment so much as it is preoccupied by the selfness of the self and the otherness of others. Sinners in the hands of superbia establish their own experience as the baseline by which all others must be judged, and anyone who fails to achieve that baseline is typecast as inferior—and not just inferior but freakishly so. It's *wrong* not to be how I am. It's senseless not to have come to the understanding that I have. It's *ridiculous* not to have accomplished what I've accomplished. I'm normal; the rest of you fall short.

Superbia sometimes manifests itself in the cockiness Peter displayed when he promised never to leave or forsake Jesus, but such arrogance doesn't necessarily bubble up to the surface of a superbian consciousness. I don't go around trumpeting my superior attitude of servanthood, for example, and I dismiss attempts by others to celebrate it. To call atten-tion to myself, to dwell on my particular areas of giftedness, to indulge the praise of others—people who do such things are morally compro-mised, to my way of thinking. I will have none of it. I will be content to know that I have served where I could, and I will only privately scorn those weaker Christians who fail to serve where they could.

Oops—I did it again. Superbia is insidious because it infects our worldview. We find our way through our days at least in part by our sense of superbia. It's a preventative coping mechanism, so to speak. We don't need to be relieved of superbia; we need to be delivered from it.

It's odd in our day and age to think of an inordinate sense of self-regard as the most subversive sin plaguing the church. People are more likely to struggle with low self-esteem than high self-esteem, aren't they? Western culture actually recognized a crisis of self-esteem in the late twentieth century that continues to afflict us. People actually *do* think too little of themselves. Countless children are devastated by the teasing and bullying they experience at school and the belittling and terrorizing they experience at home. Countless young women are driven to destructive behavior in attempts to perfect or punish their imperfect bodies. Countless men and women are dehumanized by new technologies that render them incompetent or, worse, nonessential. Countless spouses find that they can't measure up to the romantic ideals propagated in film and television. Surely the sin of self-esteem must be rooted in its lack rather than its abundance.

Superbia is subtle, though. The tragedies wreaked when people and impersonal forces whittle away at our self-esteem notwithstanding, superbia kicks in to help us cope. We rewrite ourselves into the drama we find ourselves in so that we, the sufferer, are the hero—whether that hero be epic or tragic. People who are intimidated by technology blame the "stupid computer" when things don't go as they hoped. Resentful spouses demonize romantic ideals as sentimental emotionalism and fantasize about less-demanding relationships. Marginalized young people revise themselves as misunderstood heroes, like Peter Parker/Spider-Man, or as avenging angels, like the Virginia Tech killer.

ME-VILLE

Superbia is subtle, but it has powerful outcomes. Individuals, relationships, systems, and cultures all suffer its effects. Superbia is the ground of our learned being, the garbage chute we've retreated into, like Luke and Leia and Han and Chewie on the Death Star. We turn to superbia to protect ourselves from the onslaught of a difficult world, but our refuge threatens to crush us, to destroy us.

The word *superbia* sounds to me like a place—like suburbia or
Albania or Utopia. I like to call that place Me-Ville—a kind of suburb
to the city of God. The fifth-century bishop Augustine of Hippo articulated the concept of the city of God after the imperial city of Rome was
devastated by pagan Carthage. Augustine addressed the cultural confusion that would follow any such encounter, the same sort of cultural
confusion that followed on the heels of the attacks on the Pentagon and
New York's World Trade Center in 2001. We're a Christian nation, aren't
we? We're doing God's work throughout the world, aren't we? Why,
then, did this happen?

Rome was, technically I suppose by then, a Christian empire,
but as Augustine was quick to point out, that's not how things
work. There's the kingdom that God reigns over, and there's the
kingdom that we assert in our everyday lives. They're commingled
in the way that the city of Chicago and its suburbs, for example, are
commingled. The suburbs thrive at least in part because of their
proximity to the city, but they would never dream of allowing
Chicago's mayor to tell them what to do. The suburbs fancy themselves distinct from the city, surrounding it and keeping it
contained; meanwhile, in the thrust of history Chicago keeps growing and expanding and asserting its influence.

Similarly the Roman Empire owed much of its strength and
longevity to the grace of God, but when it came down to giving God
total reign, Rome effectively said no, thank you. It continued to fiddle
around with its fantasies of autonomy; meanwhile, the city of God continued to grow—even as Rome suffered its defeat.

What happens to empires happens to us as well. We're moving happily through our lives, telling God we love him; but meanwhile our
universe revolves around us, and we act accordingly, promoting our own

agenda, pronouncing judgment on people and circumstances based on how we're affected.

Inevitably our agenda doesn't go as planned; the people we've judged wind up winning while we wind up losing. Our empire of self crumbles, and we're left to wonder in the rubble: What about me?

Sometimes in those moments we come to the realization that we're living in the wrong kingdom. The kingdom of God is firmly established because it's the place where our God reigns. Me-Ville is not. Me-Ville is where superbia reigns; it's a place from which we must escape.

ESCAPE FROM SUPERBIA

This book will look for escape routes. We are being called out of Me-Ville and onto a journey toward our true home in the city of God. Peter will be a guide for us because, as we will learn from the Scriptures, he's well acquainted with superbia and is also well acquainted with the path Jesus leads us on toward God's city. By God's grace, as we travel with Peter, we'll recognize our own vulnerabilities to self-absorption, and we'll hear God's Spirit speaking not to Peter but to us, whispering something very much like, "This is the way; walk in it."

The city of God is a place out in the open, with never-closing gates—quite different from the land we find ourselves locked inside. Such a different environment calls for different living—free living in place of confinement. But living free carries its own cost. We grow accustomed to controlled surroundings, rigid boundaries; removing those controls and subverting those boundaries can be an awkward process. At the same time, there are boundaries that were not constructed by us but given to us by One who knows us better. To transgress these boundaries, even by accident, can be painful and can send us scampering back to the safe ground of our superbian prison. However safe life in Me-Ville seems, we must take again and again on faith that it is a life not ultimately worth living because it is a life that will not extend past our death.

Mapping out our escape from superbia will involve coming to terms with where we are—recognizing the way that superbia has already infected our outlook and our relationships. It will involve coming to terms with who we have become and how we have fallen short of who we could be.

Our deliverance will also involve training our eyes on God and learning to see life unfiltered by the veneer we live under in Me-Ville. Jesus takes our place not only in our suffering but also in our assessment of what is true, honorable, just, pure, pleasing, commendable, excellent, and praiseworthy. Our way out of ourselves will involve Jesus coming to us and displacing us.

Outside of Me-Ville the fog clears, and we can get a better sense of how we can live more in step with the plans God has made for us. Having positioned ourselves in right relation to Christ, we can live more humbly and, simultaneously, more fully.

In Me-Ville we tend to see other people as, at best, tools or toys or, at worst, threats to get rid of as quickly as possible. En route to the city of God, however, we can learn to relate to others in ways that don't ask too much or too little of them. We can serve, and we can accept the service of others.

We are never far from the land we are leaving. We need to train ourselves in the way of Jesus, and we need to learn how to recover our way when we stray back into the land of Me-Ville. Each chapter then will feature a section called "Escape Routes" to focus in on practical ways, when we find ourselves slipping back into superbia, to get back on the road to the city of God.

The escape from Me-Ville is difficult and menacing because along the way we are made to feel incredibly vulnerable. At times we'll feel as though we're falling back; at times we'll feel as though we're going nowhere. But as we endure, we will discover that the city of God has been all around us all along, biding its time, silently preparing the walls of Me-Ville to come crashing down. If we are patient with ourselves, with our neighbors, and with our God, we'll discover the Promised Land right beneath our feet.

THE HIGH COST OF LIVING IN ME-VILLE

I got married recently. To my niece. It was her idea; I just went along with it. She was five at the time, over at my house with her parents and her brother and her sister, and she decided it was high time she and I got hitched. And my niece is stubborn; I knew she would not take no for an answer. So I said yes.

We didn't have an officiant, of course, so the wedding could hardly be considered official. I figured if we're going to pretend, why not do it up right? So rather than wed ourselves, we re-created the most famous impulse wedding I could think of on short notice: the wedding of Britney Spears and Kevin Federline. I played the part of K-Fed; my niece, to my brother's great chagrin, played the part of Britney.

Britney—in case you happened to discover this book in a postapocalyptic twenty-second-century church library—was a bubble-pop music sensation in the early part of the third millennium AD. Her career was at least temporarily sidetracked by a series of bad decisions including an hours-long marriage to a family friend (Jason Alexander) and an affair that would lead to marriage and two children (and a reality television series) with a man whose child by another mother hadn't been born yet (that would be K-Fed). Britney went on to redefine the party scene as a tragicomic event, attacking a car with an umbrella, shaving her head, and leaving the scene of a car accident. Perhaps you can understand my brother's concern.

Federline (who, we were eventually led to believe, was the responsible one) was an accomplished dancer for touring bubble-pop musicians such as Britney, but his real dream was to be a media sensation. Having Britney as a wife (and a television costar) opened considerable doors to K-Fed, clearing the way for him to experiment with acting (minor roles in film and on television) and rapping (his first album, *Playing with Fire,* dropped in October 2006). By the time my niece and I reenacted the Britney/K-Fed wedding, Britney had filed for divorce, and K-Fed had become (at least for the moment) a professional wrestler. His album failed, several of his tour dates were canceled, and he was ultimately named by *Star* magazine and British television, among other media outlets, one of the ten most annoying people of 2006.

Now, my niece and I weren't invited to the Britney/K-Fed wedding, so re-creating the event took some imagination. My niece, fortunately, has been protected from such silliness in her young life, so she simply pretended to be a bride, but I took my role seriously. I put a baseball cap on my head, cocked to the side. I slung an oversized coat around my waist and elbows. I slouched. I smirked. And I asserted myself unapologetically. K-Fed, I imagined, would mark his wedding not with the traditional "I do" or "To thee I pledge my troth" but with a bold-faced boast: "I'm Kevin Federline! I'm important, yo!"

Why do I share this story? I'm trying to remember.... Oh yes. I share this story because about a month after my niece and I were married, my brother called to inform me that my niece and my other niece and probably, once he learns to talk, my nephew have adopted a new catchphrase: "I'm important, yo!" They shout it over and over and over again, to my great amusement and my brother's great chagrin.

When small children learn to say, "I'm important, yo!" it's cute. It's also significant, because they *are* important. At the birth of the world, the Bible dares to suggest, God "created human beings in his own image." He went on to assign them great importance in the created order: "Fill the earth and govern it. Reign over the fish in the sea, the birds in the sky, and all the animals that scurry along the ground" (Gen. 1:27–28 NLT). Little children are important because they are human beings, and human beings are important because they are made in the image of God and bear a responsibility, in keeping with their divine likeness, to the kingdom of God.

The danger comes when small children, or grown adults, say, "I'm important, yo!" over and over and over again. Somewhere in that repetition their sense of significance morphs into something more sinister: self-absorption. Welcome to *Me-Ville.*

SUPERBIA = SELF-ABSORPTION

Imagine a young couple, leading a life of relative leisure in an idyllic garden setting. Let's call them, say, Adam and Eve. They're told at the beginning of their life together that they're important, and they're given a substantial but eminently manageable job description, complete with all the resources they'll ever need. And then they set out to enjoy a life of abundance together. Mark Twain imagined one such day in the life of our heroine, Eve, trying to share her sense of significance with a parrot. She writes in her diary,

> Polly … is gay and happy and impudent, and talks and laughs and screeches all the time. But after all, he is something

of a disappointment, he cares so little for elevated conversation, and his range of subjects is so limited. Another defect—he
repeats himself too much. This is a vulgarity. It indicates a low
order of mentality, also indifferent cultivation. I would not
judge him unjustly, yet in candor I am forced to say I believe he
lacks spirituality.... Yesterday when I spoke with strong emo-
tion, and said "How majestic is the universe, how noble the
design, how spacious, how impressive, how ..." he broke in
with a hoarse shriek, followed by his odious laugh, then
stormed out a string of strange words which instinct told me
were not nice, and demanded a cracker.[1]

It's imagined, of course, but it makes you think: How does one person, even two people, with no prior history to draw on, make sense of
the different abilities of different creatures? Given their well-developed
sense of their own importance, how do they measure the importance of
everything else—made before them but placed under their care? For
that matter, how do they make sense of one another?

Simply put, they judge everything in comparison to how they understand themselves. And they understand themselves as important. Yo.

It's almost impossible to imagine ourselves into that setting because
of the world we live in. Self-worth has run a whirlwind cycle in recent
decades. The reality of God came into question philosophically in the
late nineteenth century when Friedrich Nietzsche declared God dead
at the hands of his creation. With God's lights out, the theory went, the
world plunged into darkness. The question took on stark dimensions in
the years that followed as a world war was eclipsed by a global economic
crisis and a second world war, one in which entire people groups—
including God's "chosen people," the Jews—faced a very real possibility

of extinction. The war ended with a strong punctuation mark in the first two atomic bombs, leaving hundreds of thousands dead in two instants. Maybe God is dead, philosophers wondered; maybe he never lived in the first place, others considered. Maybe we're a meandering step on an evolutionary journey dictated by random events and mathematical possibilities. Maybe we're not that important. Whoa.

Social psychologist Jean Twenge, in her book *Generation Me*, suggests that the decades following this philosophical self-doubt nursed a self-esteem crisis that in the wake of the Vietnam era reared its ugly head:

The Coopersmith Self-Esteem Inventory, a scale written specifically for children [revealed that] during the 1970s— when the nation's children shifted from the late Baby Boom to the early years of GenX—kids' self-esteem declined, probably because of societal instability. Rampant divorce, a wobbly economy, soaring crime rates, and swinging singles culture made the 1970s a difficult time to be a kid. The average child in 1979 scored lower than 81% of kids in the mid-1960s.

A strong concern for the emotional health of children in the wake of this cultural self-doubt led to a systemwide commitment to training people in self-esteem.

Research on programs to boost self-esteem first blossomed in the 1980s, and the number of psychology and education journal articles devoted to self-esteem doubled between the 1970s and 1980s. Journal articles on self-esteem increased another 52% during the 1990s, and the number of

books on self-esteem doubled over the same time. Generation
Me is the first generation raised to believe that everyone
should have high self-esteem.[2]

That doesn't mean, of course, that everybody *has* high self-esteem.
Many people clearly don't. Consistently rising rates of depression suggest that countless people still think themselves unimportant, but the
parallel rise in self-injury as a habit (cutting, for instance, or various eating disorders) hints at a more insidious social problem: People with poor
self-image punish themselves for it.[3]

Society doesn't consider high self-esteem merely healthy; it consid-
ers it *noble*. If you don't see yourself as important, yo, you're seen as
upsetting the natural order. You're weird. As one person—*a pastor,* mind
you, who had taken upon himself responsibility for the spiritual health
of hundreds of young men and women—told me about damaged people: "I'll pray for them, but I'm not going to waste my time with them."

A side effect of the self-esteem movement has been this type of pan-
demic of self-importance—a general state of superbia.

OUT OF EDEN AND INTO ME-VILLE

When an individual descends into a state of superbia, individual costs
result—an unrealistic sense of the gap between self and God, an under-
appreciation of one's natural limitations—that lead to tragic outcomes
for the individual and the wider community.

GenMe trusts no one, suggesting a culture growing ever
more toward disconnection and away from close communities.
Trusting no one and relying on yourself is a self-fulfilling

prophecy in an individualistic world where the prevailing sentiment is "Do unto others before they do it unto you."[4]

Adam and Eve had one taboo—only one. No eating from one tree. They didn't eat meat, not because God told them not to, but because God had given them "whatever grows out of the ground for food" (Gen. 1:30), and that was more than enough. They didn't spend a lot of money on clothes, not because God didn't want them to have nice things, but because our idea of clothes was absurd to their way of thinking; they were clothed in the glory of God. Only one thing they didn't do because God told them not to do it: In a garden full of all kinds of vegetation, they could not eat from one tree—the Tree of Knowledge of Good and Evil.

The serpent, we're told in the story, was "the shrewdest of all the wild animals the LORD God had made" (Gen. 3:1 NLT). Shrewdness, however, when stacked against bearing the image of God, comes up short, and we may imagine the serpent resenting the trust that God had shown *them* rather than *him*. "Why would God put two such hopelessly naive people in charge of everything?!? They're not shrewd … they're morons! Why, I'd bet I could have them breaking the only rule they have to keep in a matter of minutes!"

It is embarrassing how easily Eve and Adam fell prey to the serpent's shrewdness. A few choice words about the artificial limits God had apparently placed on two people with such unbelievable potential, and they were convinced that they were important, yo, that God was killing their buzz, holding them back, bringing them down. They were spitting out seeds before they knew it.

God came by soon after that act of revolt, and he asked them where they were, which on the face of it is a weird question—where else could they possibly be? They were in Eden, the place God had put them in, but in a very real sense they were no longer in God's kingdom. Right there, under the shadow God cast, they were standing in Me-Ville.

We get a sense of the relational impact in Adam and Eve's reaction: Adam said, "The woman ... gave me the fruit." Eve said, "The serpent deceived me.... That's why I ate it" (Gen. 3:12–13 NLT). Jean Twenge would accuse Adam and Eve of "externalizing" their moral breach:

> A popular psychological scale ... measures a fundamental belief: are you in control of what happens to you, or do other people, luck, and larger forces control your fate? People who believe they are in control are "internal" (and possess "internality"); those who don't are "external." ... The average GenMe college student in 2002 had more external control beliefs than 80% of college students in the early 1960s. External control beliefs increased about 50% between the 1960s and the 2000s.[5]

Adam and Eve each denied their own responsibility when confronted by God because they saw themselves as too important to be wrong, to be weak, to be vulnerable to the shrewdness of a mere serpent. The dramatic increase in self-importance over the turn of the millennium, occurring alongside a steady increase in divorce, white-collar crime, morbid obesity, and high-profile falls from grace, smacks of a similar stink. We're too important for silly rules. We can't be expected to keep promises we made after circumstances change. Give us enough time, and we'll figure out who's really to blame for the trouble we find ourselves in. Jake Blues covered all bases when he was confronted by his ex-fiancée for skipping their wedding in the film *The Blues Brothers:*

> I ran outta gas. I had a flat tire. I didn't have enough
> money for cab fare. My tux didn't come back from the clean-
> ers. An old friend came in from outta town. Someone stole
> my car. There was an earthquake, a terrible flood, locusts. It
> wasn't my fault!! I swear to God!!

Imagine all the members of the entire human population of the earth desperately trying to cover their own butts—on constant lookout for a scapegoat. That's Adam and Eve, just past their moment of weakness. That's you and me and everybody else, in our moments of weakness. That's superbia, and it has an impact on the culture we inhabit.

WILL YOU ASCEND TO THE HEIGHTS?

Within thirteen generations of Adam and Eve, and after a colorful history of murder, polygamy, and such vile immoral behavior that God virtually started over, the entire human race finally got down to business: "Let's build a great city for ourselves with a tower that reaches into the sky. This will make us famous" (Gen. 11:4 NLT) Keep in mind: This was *everybody;* they already all knew each other. So becoming famous was a bit superfluous. But becoming famous is the holy grail for people steeped in superbia. Consider the sad tale of William Hung.

American Idol, the mother of all reality shows, is at its core a singing competition. Contestants are, theoretically, everyday people off the street who happen to have a world-class voice and a knack for singing bubble-pop. Only other people, luck, and larger forces have kept them from already making themselves known on the contemporary music scene. Each season begins with a showcase of the people who have worked up the moxie to declare themselves publicly as idol-worthy.

Among them, in 2004, was William Hung, whose audition is now the stuff of legend. In the middle of a painful rendition of the bubble-pop song "She Bang," Hung was interrupted by one of the show's three judges, Simon Cowell: "You can't sing; you can't dance. So what do you want me to say?"

Hung's hopes for a career in music had been shot down. "Umm," he stammered, "I already gave my best. And I have no regrets at all." There was no need for regret, of course, because his dream of a music career was only secondary. His primary dream—the dream of all the other people waiting for their turn in front of Simon and his fellow judges, Randy Jackson and Paula Abdul, and the dream of the whole shovel-wielding human race laying the foundation for the Tower of Babel—had already been realized by William Hung. He was now famous.

Standing there, basking awkwardly in the American limelight, Hung attempted to justify himself. "You know I've had no professional training." That much was already evident, but the last moment of his televised attempt to become America's next musical idol was not the voice of reason—"You can't sing; you can't dance"—but a throwaway attempt at encouragement by Paula Abdul: "William, you're the best." *American Idol,* the ultimate judge of what is worthy of our idolatry, sent William Hung home, saying to himself, "I'm important, yo."

IT'S EASY FOR ME

It's easy for me to point out the absurdity of William Hung and Kevin Federline and Generation Me and Adam and Eve and all of Babel-onia declaring themselves important and pursuing fame as the highest end of living. I'm not them, and more important to me, they're not here. Ultimately they likely won't even be adversely affected by my ridicule of them. Even K-Fed and Hung, my two most vulnerable victims, will likely see their fame extended by virtue of people like me rambling on incessantly about how absurd their pursuit of fame is. Meanwhile I'm doing something significant: I'm writing a book, making moral judgments about what I consider noble and praiseworthy and what I consider pathetic and laughable, and suggesting to you that these moral judgments are important enough to be put in print, paid for, and read. I may even try to get your church to bring me in to give a talk about it.

There I go again, declaring myself mayor of Me-Ville. Sorry about that. Fame is a stamp of approval on the human psyche. The television show *Dirt* defined the concept bitterly when a fledgling celebrity's private life became fodder for a scandal sheet. The celebrity complained to the editor, "I just want to be an actor." The editor responded, "No, you just want to be famous. There's a big difference." For all their complaints about the unexpected consequences of fame—the highly publicized errors in judgment, the constant press of people, and the profound lack of privacy—people still strive after it as a barometer of their self-worth. The Portico Research Group assessed the culture as guilty of "creating a culture of possibility. These young people see every aspect of life as an open opportunity for self-expression and self-fulfillment."[6] My greatest fear in making my writing public, quite frankly, is not that my book won't sell or my ideas will be challenged by my critics; it's that an audience will read what I write and disregard it as insignificant. Such is the anxiety of the fame-addicted:

When success is so largely a function of youth, glamour,
and novelty, glory is more fleeting than ever, and those who
win the attention of the public worry incessantly about losing it.[7]

You can get around that anxiety, however. Fame as a personal goal,
utterly divorced from the pursuit of excellence, has become a noble
quest in a culture that buys William Hung records. Psychology professor Terry Cooper nails our collective self-regard:

> The desire to have a profound self-confidence without
> any self-development is sometimes obvious in American soci-
> ety. Self-esteem becomes a new form of entitlement. We have
> a *right* to feel good about ourselves.[8]

A. W. Tozer calls the self "so subtle … that scarcely anyone is conscious of its presence."[9] Even as we recognize that others have taken up
residence in Me-Ville, we are often dangerously close to our own slide
into it. In many cases we're already there; Me-Ville functions as a meeting place of self-important people who have measured one another and
found them lacking.

Superbia rears its ugly head when we are at our most vulnerable—
suddenly disrupted from our default self-satisfaction. You might think
of it as a staged descent:

Stage one: I congratulate myself on some random achievement or
passing prominence.

Stage two: Something embarrasses, humiliates, or scandalizes me.

Stage three: I look for someone or something to blame for what I've done.

Stage four: I look for ways to reassure myself that I'm better than everybody around me.

Cooper articulates this pattern as an example of attribution theory: "We humans tend to attribute positive behaviors to ourselves and negative behaviors to external factors. We take credit for the good things that happen to us and blame the bad things on outside considerations."[10]

RED-CARPET TREATMENT

In 2007 I became an elder at my church—the pinnacle of power for a devout Protestant layperson such as myself. The weekend before my ordination I attended two training sessions and managed to dump my cup of coffee at both meetings. This minor act of clumsiness was embarrassing enough, but it happened in front of the royal guard of our congregation, on the eve of my ordination, on the brand-new carpet.

In my case the coffee spill was a minor embarrassment, a moment of humiliation, or a scandal of the highest order—depending on how much you value carpet. If I hadn't been in stage one, I probably would have laughed it off and hoped nobody else would freak out. But I was in stage one, and suddenly I found myself in stage two; my self-congratulation had been interrupted by humiliation and potential scandal. So I looked for a way out.

Of course I blamed the coffee, which was ridiculously hot; and of course I blamed that stupid, flimsy, disposable cup. But blaming temporal, disposable objects wasn't going to cut it. I needed to figure out a way to blame the carpet. More than that, I needed to blame something with flesh and blood.

What kind of church community are we building, it came to my mind, *if people need to adapt their behavior to accommodate something as inconsequential as carpet? Do people actually think that's hospitable? Someone who needs to know Jesus is going to come in here and innocently spill a little coffee or lemonade—they'll probably get bumped by one of these thoughtless oafs here—and they'll get chased out of the building.* People were thinking way too much of that carpet, I quickly deduced. It had become an idol in our church. I was surrounded by a bunch of stinking idolaters.

Wait a minute—these stinking idolaters are the spiritual leaders of this church! My job as a new elder suddenly got much more important: I needed to save this community from itself.

Keep in mind, nobody said a word to me when I spilled the coffee. Nor did I get all prophetic on everybody, renouncing their idolatrous ways and calling them back to a spirit of humility and mission. I laughed, got a wet paper towel, and cleaned up my mess; and we all moved on. In my head, however, I was no longer simply a mildly klutzy elder; I was the salvation of my church, I daresay the salvation of my whole community. I could almost hear some random princess in a galaxy far, far away, begging, "Help me, David Zimmerman, author of two books and the youngest elder at your church; you're my only hope."

I was rewriting the story I found myself in so that I could play a better part. It's a helpful coping mechanism: Allies become enemies, heroes become bit players, heroines become damsels in distress, all in the service of our placing ourselves in the center—whether we're really hero quality or not.

Tozer sums it up nicely:

> An inward principle of self lies at the source of human
> conduct, turning everything men do into evil. To save us
> completely Christ must reverse the bent of our nature.[11]

Christ reverses the bent of our nature by leading us out of Me-Ville
and into the city of God. That act ennobles and humbles us all at the
same time because it admits of our need—we are unable to redirect ourselves, unable to fulfill the heroic needs of the story we find ourselves
in—and it brings us to a direct encounter with the Creator and Sus-
tainer of all that is seen and unseen. The way out of Me-Ville is
unavoidably through Jesus, who visits us, displaces us, delivers us, and
sets us within the bounds of his city, his community.

But before Jesus can deliver us from our own private superbia, he
must first visit us. In the next chapter we'll find Jesus in Me-Ville, and
we'll wonder what he's doing there and why we settled there in the first
place.

⬤ ESCAPE ROUTES ⬤

KNOW THYSELF

Superbia is insidious: We see it more clearly in others than we see it in ourselves. But it's there, rearing its ugly head perhaps more often than we think. This week, keep a journal of your interactions with other people—either direct interactions, people you talk to or sit next to on the train, or indirect interactions through television or film. Pay attention to what you find yourself thinking about them and what thoughts about yourself well up alongside them. Brian Mahan, author of *Forgetting Ourselves on Purpose,* calls this tendency "invidious comparison": We assess other people through the lens of ourselves, and we assess ourselves through the lens of other people. And you know, I suppose, what happens when one assesses.

Ask yourself questions such as these:

- What was my visceral reaction when I first saw this person? Was I positively or negatively inclined toward the person? Why? Was I neutral toward the person? Why might I have such a noncommittal attitude toward someone like this person?
- What points of identification did I notice with this person? In what ways are we the same or similar? Did those similarities make me feel better or worse about the person? About myself? Why?
- What points of distinction did I notice between myself and this person? Was I proud of those distinctions? Ashamed? Neutral? Why?

- If I had to assign a pecking order to myself and this person—in terms of social value or spiritual maturity or strength of character or cultural intelligence—would this person be ahead of me or behind me?

- How does my perceived status in those pecking orders affect my sense of self-worth? My feelings toward this person? My conduct toward this person?

- How hard was it to perform this exercise with people I know well? People I don't know but encounter directly? People on TV or in other media?

- Where do I see superbia in myself peeking through these encounters?

2

JESUS VISITS US IN ME-VILLE

Sometimes, I willingly confess, I am *at* church but not entirely *in* church. Sometimes my mind is still on what I watched on TV or read in the paper earlier that morning; sometimes I'm thinking about what I'd like to say to that guy over there in place of "Peace be with you." And sometimes I have pronoun trouble.

Has this ever happened to you? The music starts to a familiar tune, and your mind drifts along, enjoying a light, essentially noncommittal moment. Maybe there's a little swaying going on, and in your peripheral vision you can see a hand or two in the air, waving like they just don't care. And you decide that you don't need to look at the song book in front of you or at the giant TV screen above you, because you've been singing this song for years and you know the lyrics like the backs of your waving, noncommittal hands. So you enjoy the moment and sing right through it: "Thou, O Lord, are my heart's desire, and I long to worship me."

Wait! "Thee"—I meant "thee"!

The problem is common enough. A clever YouTube video "sells" a self-worship CD titled *It's All About Me.*[1] You can, the video suggests, sing along to great anthems of self worship such as "Now I Lift My

Name on High" and "I Exalt Me." Blame contemporary worship song-writing if you'd like, but I can trip up even on the most revered prayer in the history of Christianity: "Our Father, who art in heaven, hallowed be my name."

Wait! "Thy"—I meant "thy"!

Me-Ville is so hard to escape because it's where all our stuff is. Within Me-Ville we live and move and have our being. We work and play and socialize and exercise. Our homes, our places of work, our places of worship are all merely destination points within the universe we've organized for ourselves. It's no wonder, then, that Me-Ville invades our worship. What's remarkable, actually, is that Jesus somehow finds his way into Me-Ville to visit us.

EVERYWHERE I WANT TO BE

As a matter of fact, Me-Ville is virtually the only place we can meet Jesus. That's not to say that Me-Ville is the only place God is, but it's the place we so often find ourselves, so by extension it's the place *God* finds *us*. In actuality God is everywhere we turn:

> I can never escape from your Spirit!
>   I can never get away from your presence!
> If I go up to heaven, you are there;
>   if I go down to the grave, you are there.
> If I ride the wings of the morning,
>   if I dwell by the farthest oceans,
> even there your hand will guide me,
>   and your strength will support me.
> I could ask the darkness to hide me

and the light around me to become night—
but even in darkness I cannot hide from you.
To you the night shines as bright as day.
Darkness and light are the same to you.
(Ps. 139:7–12 NLT)

When I graduated from high school, I decided that I had graduated from church as well. I continued to do my time throughout the summer, but I knew well in advance that in the fall my relationship with Christianity would come to an end.

Then I arrived on campus and met my roommate, two years older than me, a student of the religion department. On my first night in the dorms, my roommate pulled out a bong—not the first I'd seen but a good hint at what the next six months would be like until I could find another roommate. He lit up, and between hits he asked me an odd question: "What do you think of Jesus?"

I hemmed and hawed and stuttered and muttered something about Jesus being like Superman or Spider-Man or some other superhero—certainly not God, but certainly someone special. My roommate either forgot he had asked or decided he didn't care, because the conversation took a decidedly different turn after that. I could not deny, however, that I'd had my first encounter with Jesus at college, and it was weird.

A couple of days later I met Chris, a quirky freshman outcast not unlike myself. Chris was carrying his guitar, and I was carrying my saxophone—I was on my way back from jazz ensemble auditions; he was just being a freshman—and we struck up a conversation. We quickly became fast friends, and before too long Chris started practicing evangelism on me.

Chris, it turned out, had experienced a dramatic conversion earlier that year and was now busily teaching himself how to share his faith with other people. I was a guinea pig, as I understood it: He told me what kind of person he had been, what Jesus had done for him, and what kind of person he was now. I listened and nodded and congratulated him on the strength of his presentation. I didn't convert or anything, and we moved on from that conversation to more productive things like hitting on girls. But in the back of my mind was the growing notion that people in Illinois sure did like to talk about Jesus.

Why would Jesus bother to leave Des Moines and travel all the way to Bloomington just to track down little old me? That's one way of looking at it, of course: I'm so important, yo, that the God of the universe would drop what he's doing to keep me on his viewscreen. But my roommate was from central Illinois, and Chris was from Chicago, and as it turned out, there were other folks on campus from other parts of the country—even other parts of the world—who had experienced similar encounters with the same Jesus. By the end of my freshman year, I had studied the Bible regularly with Chris and some other friends; I had been exposed to contemporary Christian music by John, a pastor's kid from southern Illinois; and I had followed some girls to various churches over a string of Sundays as research for their Introduction to Religion class. (I wasn't in the class, but I was into the girls.) Jesus, it seemed, was everywhere I wanted to be—and even in places I no longer was or hadn't been yet.

What became painfully obvious was that Jesus wasn't a lapdog meekly trying to plant himself on my lap. Jesus in fact represents the God of the universe, who is too big to be contained in one space, too big to fit in one measly lap. Solomon put it this way, in so somber a moment as the dedication of the temple of the Lord: "Will God really dwell on earth? The heavens, even the highest heaven, cannot contain you. How much less this temple I have built!" (1 Kings 8:27 NIV).

Solomon said this, of course, just moments after a cloud of smoke—"the glory of the LORD"—had filled that same temple. In the consecration of the temple, Solomon was giving voice to an intuitive paradox of the Jewish faith: An unapproachable God chooses to abide with his people.

THE GREAT CLOUD OF UNCARING

The New Testament asserts that God dwells in unapproachable light (1 Tim. 6:16)—which is not to say, necessarily, that God is sitting somewhere that would burn out our retinas if we dared to steal a glance. It means that God is so unfathomable to us as to be effectively unseeable. The same concept is declared poetically in the Old Testament:

> The LORD … wraps himself in light as with a garment.
> (Ps. 104:1–2 NIV)

> His way is in the whirlwind and the storm,
>   and clouds are the dust of his feet. (Nah. 1:3 NIV)

> He made darkness his canopy around him—
>   the dark rain clouds of the sky.
> Out of the brightness of his presence
>   bolts of lightning blazed forth. (2 Sam. 22:12–13 NIV)

There you have it: brightness clothed in darkness, bolts of lightning blazing out of dark clouds. Keep your distance.

God is awe-inspiring in his brilliance, in his bigness, in his Otherness. That's what compelled the writers of Scripture to come up with such stunning descriptions of him. But to a person trapped in Me-Ville, this kind of overwhelming greatness doesn't inspire awe so much as it creates anxiety. A God who created everything and who watches over his creation, utterly unknowable to us, is kind of scary. The only comparisons we can make in the abstract are negative—spies, voyeurs, fascist governments. Check out the lyrics to a song from the 1990s, sung in chapel services across the country: "God is watching us. God is watching us. God is watching us from a distance." Imagine a smooth, matronly voice, lilting and wafting as the singer sways serenely, accompanied by string instruments. Now, put down this book for a minute, go to your computer, type each sentence of those lyrics, and see how you feel. Go ahead; I'll wait. (Don't check your e-mail, though; I don't have all day.)

...

When we're hunched over a computer in isolation, and the words are stripped of the strings and the pastel colors, those lyrics are distressing:

God is watching us.
God is watching us.
God is watching us.

Somewhere undetected a higher power is spying on us, judging us, deciding our fate. The only comfort comes from identifying this voyeuristic God's vantage point: God isn't close by; he's far off, watching us from a distance. That's pretty cold comfort. I'm reminded of a skit a friend of mine once performed around Christmastime. Dressed in an

overcoat and fedora, carrying a violin case, my friend spoke in a menacing, mafioso voice:

> You betta watch out,
> You betta not cry.
> You betta not pout—
> I'm tellin' you why:
> Santa Claus is comin' to town.
>
> He sees you when you're sleepin'
> He knows when you're awake.

Taken out of its familiar context—peppy music, cheery voices—
the reassuring, endearing idea of Santa Claus becomes a thinly veiled
threat. Our idea of God is exactly the same, with one small difference:
God is real.

The deists of the eighteenth century, recognizing the problem of
managing a God who knows all and sees all, softened this oppressive
image: God was not a fascist despot passing secret judgment but a kindly
yet dispassionate watchmaker, who winds up his watch and then
watches it wind down. This God loses his sting; we're free to live our
lives however we like, while a pleasant old gentleman God, whose vital-
ity has long since passed, contents himself to merely observe us at play.

This idea of God, which hits its stride in the song "From a Distance" quoted above, has proved to be a significant force in American
religion and a fitting God of Me-Ville. This God offers great consola-
tion to his adherents—no matter how bad things get, from God's
perspective it's all working out just fine. Under Me-Ville's understanding of God, we can even dismiss evidence that suggests we're making a

mess of things, creating a world that any god worth his salt would judge and condemn. Take a look at some more of our song of insane rambling from before:

> From a distance we all have enough,
> and no one is in need.
> There are no guns, no bombs, and no disease
> No hungry mouths to feed.

This obvious mischaracterization of reality would be possible only when an ambivalent God watches his creation without intervening, when people willingly delude themselves in order to make their passage from day to day smoother. We gladly approach the God of Me-Ville in worship because he can't be bothered to approach us in rebuke. Meanwhile the God of the Bible, wrapped in unapproachable light, lies outside the boundaries of Me-Ville, outside our field of vision.

HE PARTED THE HEAVENS

The great thing about this unapproachable God, however, is that he does approach us, and in so doing, he reveals to us enough of his character that we can draw some conclusions about who he is and what he intends for us. The same God who wraps himself in light in Psalm 104 blesses all of creation by maintaining it:

> These all look to you
> > to give them their food at the proper time.
> When you give it to them,
> > they gather it up;

when you open your hand,

they are satisfied with good things....

When you send your Spirit,

they are created,

and you renew the face of the earth.

(vv. 27–28, 30 NIV)

God may be stormy and unapproachable in Nahum 1, but he's also actively aware of and responsive to our needs:

The LORD is good,

a refuge in times of trouble.

He cares for those who trust in him....

Look, there on the mountains,

the feet of one who brings good news,

who proclaims peace! (vv. 7, 15 NIV)

Despite how he ordains himself in 2 Samuel 22, God shows up in response to David's prayer: "He parted the heavens and came down" (v. 10 NIV).

Even as Solomon is acknowledging the absurdity of giving God a home, we witness God entering the temple because God cares about his creation—enough to get his feet dirty as he enters into our existence, taking on the challenges of being a God to a people who are often too caught up in themselves to pay attention to him.

"They go from one sin to another;

they do not acknowledge me,"

declares the LORD. (Jer. 9:3 NIV)

This is, apparently, not a new problem. Long before Jean Twenge wrote *Generation Me,* long before sociologist Christopher Lasch wrote *The Culture of Narcissism*—long before some anonymous Greek myth-maker crafted the tale of Narcissus staring so long at his own reflection that he was transformed into a weed—people have been too caught up in themselves even to acknowledge the Lord of heaven and earth. And so the challenge for would-be disciples living in Me-Ville is to notice God when he comes.

MY PRIVATE UNIVERSE

The gospel of John opens with a poetic assertion of Jesus' divinity: The Word of God who is fully God took on flesh. Not that it made God's task of revealing himself and his will to the world any easier.

> He was in the world,
>> the world was there through him,
>> and yet the world didn't even notice.
> He came to his own people,
>> but they didn't want him. (John 1:10–11)

John's gospel sums up the extraordinary event of God visiting earth in very pragmatic language, revealing that God's pursuit of us is not dependent on our interest in him: "The Word became flesh and blood, and moved into the neighborhood" (John 1:14).

Of course moving into a neighborhood is generally more momentous for the new resident than the current occupants. When my wife and I moved into our neighborhood, we didn't meet anybody for a long time, with the exception of the precocious six-year-old who wanted to know if we had any kids her age (we didn't). It took a surprisingly long time to meet her parents—our next-door neighbors to the north—or the woman to the south with whom we shared a driveway, or anyone else for that matter. Nor did we go far out of our way to introduce ourselves to them. To intrude on the privacy of our neighbors' homes seemed to us (and apparently to them) something that good people don't do. Only a kid who didn't know any better would be so bold.

As a result we felt the tiniest bit unwelcome, unsafe, in our new neighborhood. Eventually I invited our next-door neighbor to the south (the one who shares our driveway) into our home for a visit. She walked through quickly, uncomfortably, noting that our houses were essentially mirror copies of each other, with the exception of our family room, which had been added on after the fact. She also pointed out that our neighbors to the north, along with several other houses on our block, had been built off the same blueprints. I hadn't noticed that. She excused herself soon after that, but the ice had broken, and before long she was feeding our cats for us and shoveling the driveway with us.

For a while I was emboldened by my experience with my next-door neighbor to the south, and so I would occasionally venture a chat over the fence with my neighbor to the north, who coincidentally had the same first name as me and who had a dog that needed feeding while his family was out of town over the coming weekend. I even crossed the street once or twice, chatting briefly with the guy who meticulously waters and weeds his lawn. His neighbor to the south, who worked out at the same gym as I did, showed up spontaneously on my driveway one morning during a blizzard to help dig me out. The neighborhood seemed to be coming together, feeling more like home.

Then the house a couple of doors down sold, and a new family moved in. My wife and I, determined as we were to make their transition into the neighborhood smoother than our own, baked some cookies. I walked them over to the house and tapped on the door—probably more quietly than I meant to—and nobody answered. I tapped again—though not any louder than before—and waited a minute or so for a response. Nobody came to the door, so I dropped the plate of cookies and went home and unconsciously determined that from here on out I would mind my own business.

THE SUM OF OURSELVES

Why is it so inherently awkward to meet someone new? Undoubtedly because of any number of factors, of course, but one of them is certainly the fact that anything new is a disruption of the status quo.

The status quo becomes incredibly important in the context of a machine we can't ourselves control, which is where most of us find ourselves. Our economic stability is determined by an elite few in the upper echelons of multinational corporations manipulating markets and employing (and occasionally laying off) thousands of workers at a stretch. We can't individually control the destiny of where we work, so we inflate our self-understanding and reduce our professional universe to a more manageable size as an act of psychological self-preservation. Lasch writes:

> For all his inner suffering, the narcissist has many traits that make for success in bureaucratic institutions, which put a premium on the manipulation of interpersonal relations, discourage the formation of deep personal attachments, and at the same time provide the narcissist with the approval he needs in order to validate his self-esteem.[2]

We figure out how to occupy our time and how to fill our space by thinking in patterns: Mondays I work on this and call on him; Tuesdays I call on her and work on that. And we're rewarded for it: In the movie *Office Space* one of hundreds of anonymous workers is singled out as management material after being inadvertently hypnotized not to care about anyone or anything but his own sense of inner peace. The movie has proved successful because the concept is so familiar: When we figure out how to work the system, and all the people in it, we are rewarded with more substantial titles and more office space. A happy side effect of the turn inward is that the annals of power are reduced in our minds to an abstraction, some far-off other watching us only from a distance, which we consequently don't have to deal with.

That's work. Home life isn't much different, however. Constantly expanding cosmopolises constitute home to 80 percent of the three-hundred-million-strong U.S. population, according to the 2000 census. Growth in those communities has been often more reactive than proactive, so that major population centers are characterized by sprawl—citizens trying to get as far away as possible from one another without losing bragging rights of calling their metropolis home. Asking people at my school where they came from, for example, was a two-tiered interview:

> Question 1: Where do you live?
> Answer 1: Chicago.
> Question 2: What part of Chicago?
> Answer 2: Oh, about ninety minutes out, near the Missis-
> sippi River.

I used to make fun of those people until I moved to Chicago

myself—or should I say, moved to the western suburbs, about forty minutes out.

Mentioning the specific region or suburb of a metropolitan area is, of course, pointless. The names blend together as much as the streets and the strip malls do. When you're not sure where you are in Chicagoland, for example, combine a body of water with some other natural phenomenon: Lake Forest, perhaps, or Oak Brook. You're probably not far off. Goods and services meander in and out of these subcommunities as casually and disconnectedly as commuters and homeowners do, so chances are the bulk of a person's life is invested outside of the person's neighborhood. Andy Crouch points out the relative absurdity of contemporary neighborhood living—at least from the point of view of someone living before cheap flights and frequent career changes:

> I live in Massachusetts, and I can literally reach out of
> my window and touch the wall of my neighbor's house.
> There are days when my neighbor and I walk out to the curb
> at the same time to fetch our papers or take out our trash,
> and we don't talk—barely acknowledge each other. And yet
> often I will wake up in the morning, kiss my wife and kids,
> and fly across the country to have lunch with a friend.[3]

The home becomes a refuge rather than a hub; we go there when we've finished doing what needs doing, seeing who needs seeing. Once we're there, our day is done.

In such an environment, neighbors aren't personal so much as they are utilitarian. To my north is a family of five, and I must watch them to ensure that they don't ruin my grass with their bikes and I don't run over their toys with my car. To my south is the owner of a snowblower;

I must befriend her in case the weather turns ugly.[4] We share a driveway, so I must be prepared to negotiate the whens and hows of resurfacing our common blacktop. The guy across the street sets the bar for lawn-care, so if I don't want to earn a bad reputation, I will mow when he mows, weed when he weeds. Our neighborhood is reduced to patterns and quirks, and I am reduced, in the jaded words of a young Thomas Merton before entering the monastery, to "another inert member of the middle class."[5]

The objectifying of the people nearest us is an example of contemporary hedonism, which, according to Christopher Lasch, "originates not in the pursuit of pleasure but in a war of all against all, in which even the most intimate encounters become a form of mutual exploitation."[6] Jean Vanier sees it as a sort of psychological safeguard:

> To give food to a beggar who knocks on the door can be quite an easy thing to do. But if he keeps coming back—with his friends—what then do we do? We can become totally lost and insecure.... We all want to turn away from anything that reveals the failure, pain, sickness, and death beneath the brightly painted surface of our ordered lives. Civilization is, at least in part, about pretending that things are better than they are.[7]

The song "The Way We Get By" by Spoon bitterly acknowledges the lack of meaning characterized in the life we've settled for:

> We put faith in our concerns—
> fall in love to drown our misery.
> We believe in the sum of ourselves.

JESUS HONORS AND THREATENS US BY HIS VISIT

Imagine Jesus moving into such a neighborhood, since that, in effect, is what he did. You might or might not, as a courtesy, tap lightly on his door in order to drop off some cookies or some other socially acceptable token of welcome and offer enough small talk about his background or yours to establish your reputation as a hospitable, neighborly type of person. Jesus, by contrast, I think, would act less like me and more like my six-year-old neighbor to the north, calling urgently over the fence; banging excitedly on the door; wanting to come in and get to know you, see how you decorate your refuge, gauge how you fill your time.

The little booklet *My Heart—Christ's Home* imagines that scenario for us. Written decades ago, it presumes a different type of neighborhood, a community where neighbors actually did expect to get to know one another. Jesus is recognized instantly, welcomed in eagerly, and shown around proudly; the narrator is not surprised but nevertheless honored to have Jesus as a guest. Only gradually does he realize that when Jesus comes, everything must change.

Contemporary reality is different. If Jesus came to my world, I expect he would discover that I, like the rest of the world, "didn't even notice ... didn't want him" (John 1:10–11). Once we had made the proper introductions, of course, I might feel differently, probably conflicted. On the one hand, this guest is important; this guest improves my social standing. To have the Son of God in my home tells the world that I am important, yo, that my home is sacred.

Of course I've already decided that my home is sacred, so to the degree that Jesus enters my home and exposes it to the judgment of a holy God, he becomes an immediate threat. He's no longer watching from a distance, like the grandfatherly God I've come to appreciate; he's now in my face. I show him my kitchen, perhaps, and he asks why I fill my life with so many things that add bulk but don't nourish. I take him to my living room, and he asks why all the chairs face the television instead of each other. I take him to my bedroom, and he just stares at me, saying nothing. My private universe is threatened; the sum of myself is under scrutiny. It's enough to make me wonder if theologian Dietrich Bonhoeffer was right: "There are only two ways possible of encountering Jesus: man must die or he must put Jesus to death."[8]

JESUS IS PRO-ME

Here's where faith steps in. The difference between Jesus the dubious guest and Jesus the Lord and Savior is that Jesus is *pro-me,* a Latin phrase that translates roughly as "pro-me."[9] Now, that phrase may sound a bit too cheeky, as though Jesus is sitting on the couch, watching the Super Bowl of our lives on his HDTV, spilling nacho cheese all over himself as he cheers us on to the prize of being named "most valuable player." But the idea that Jesus is "pro-me" is much more substantial than that. Jesus is fully God, but by his incarnation he is also fully human—the image of that effectively invisible God. He has become in flesh what we've read of God in the pages of the Bible: a friend of sinners, a deliverer from all kinds of evil, and a teacher thoroughly invested in our well-being. Jesus is in fact so pro-me that he in effect *becomes* me:

- He takes on flesh, which necessitates that he surrender power.
- He takes on a commitment to our relationship that is almost entirely one-sided.
- He takes on himself sin that belongs to me.

• He takes on death, which I am vulnerable to but which
  could never approach him without his consent.

In his book *New Seeds of Contemplation* Thomas Merton dis-
cusses God's approach to salvation in language that reflects Jesus'
pro-me orientation:

> [Salvation] reflects God's own infinite concern for man,
> God's love and care for man's inmost being, God's love for
> all that is His own in man, His son. It is not only human
> nature that is "saved" by the divine mercy, but above all the
> human person.... We must be saved above all from that
> abyss of confusion and absurdity which is our own worldly
> self. The person must be rescued from the individual. The
> free son of God must be saved from the conformist slave of
> fantasy, passion and convention.[10]

Out of his love for me, Jesus becomes like me so he can save me
from me. Try saying that three times fast.

Simon Peter knew all about the God of the Bible; he did and all his
friends did. He had even met Jesus and been impressed with his teaching and even his ability to heal the sick. But that had precious little to
do with the day-to-day events of his life. He was too busy catching fish,
tending to his family, keeping his head above water to get caught up in
the ethereal ramblings of the rabbis and Pharisees and Sadducees of his
day. He didn't get involved in the political maneuvering or nationalis-
tic fervor of the Zealots; all that was maybe a bit over his head. He was
a quiet boy who kept to himself.

One day a crowd gathered around Jesus to listen to him teach where

Simon Peter was trying to work. It must have been a mild nuisance, having the pious posturing of this itinerant teacher intrude on his otherwise quiet, fishnet-cleaning end to his night of fishing. He probably heard some if not all of what Jesus had to say and likely was impressed—they'd met before, after all—but on this day he kept himself out of it, minding his own business, following his own well-established patterns.

Then Jesus invited himself into Simon Peter's boat like some rambunctious, overreaching six-year-old. That's not how it works, you know: Teachers teach, fishers fish, and never the twain shall meet. But Jesus' request initiated a cultural protocol that Simon Peter simply had to follow, to protect his reputation as a neighborly fellow, to guard his future social utility. So Simon Peter let Jesus into his boat, at which point Jesus started bossing him around.

"Push out into deep water," Jesus said. "Let your nets out for a catch," he instructed. Grrrr. The boat was already docked; the nets were freshly cleaned after a night of catching nothing. Stick to teaching, Jesus. This battle of wills challenged not only the boundaries of Simon Peter's private universe but also the notion of who controlled his life. He had two possible responses: He could put to death his own agenda, or he could put Jesus in his place.

In a socially brilliant move—one of the few we see him actually pull off—Simon Peter hedges his bets. "Master," he says, with perhaps a hint of sarcasm, "we've been fishing hard all night and haven't caught even a minnow." *Get it, Teacher? Leave fishing to the fishermen!* "But if you say so, I'll let out the nets." *See that, crowd? I'm accommodating; I have respect for the religious authorities; I even have a wee bit of faith.*

Simon Peter is playing the martyr, a social archetype that masks self-regard in self-disregard. Puritan John Cotton recognized the many shapes superbia takes as we strive to brand both our successes and our failures with a personal nobility, as we assert ourselves as heroes whether we are winning or losing: "It is the same act of unbeleefe, that makes a man murmure in crosses, which puffes him up in prosperity."[11]

Simon Peter expected a cross of sorts in this moment, but Jesus makes him indisputably prosperous: "a huge haul of fish, straining the nets past capacity" (Luke 5:4–6). All his socialization is then thrown out the window, and Simon Peter is left to make a confession; in so doing he shows that as much as we might want to be delivered from Me-Ville, a part of us will cling to it: "Master, leave. I'm a sinner and can't handle this holiness. Leave me to myself."

Jesus won't leave; the miraculous catch of fish is a gift from Jesus to Peter, but it's also a demonstrative act: I'm for you, Peter; I'm with you. And with me with you, everything changes.

In the book *Christ the Center* Dietrich Bonhoeffer distinguishes between a conception of a God who is—a grandfatherly God who minds his own business and leaves us to ourselves—and a God who is *pro-me.*

> Christ is Christ, not just for himself, but in relation to me. His being Christ is his being for me, *pro me.…* Christ can never be thought of as being for himself, but only in relation to me. That in turn means that Christ can only be thought of existentially.… As Luther says, "There is therefore a distinction between when God is there and when he is there for you" (Luther, *Weimarer Ausgabe* 23, 152). It is not only useless to contemplate a Christ for himself, it is even godless.[12]

Jesus in the flesh, in the boat, in our face, affirms what we've been told on paper, what's been handed down to us throughout the whole history of the people of God: The God who created us is for us, and we

can no more disregard the God who created us than we can disregard
our very selves.

> You were shown these things so that you might know
> that the LORD is God; besides him there is no other. From
> heaven he made you hear his voice to discipline you. On
> earth he showed you his great fire, and you heard his words
> from out of the fire.…
> Acknowledge and take to heart this day that the LORD is
> God in heaven above and on the earth below. There is no
> other. (Deut. 4:35–36, 39 NIV)

MYSPACE—CHRIST'S HOME PAGE

Peter dropped his nets and took off after Jesus because he could see
where Jesus was going. We don't have such luxury today: Jesus is not in
our physical face, and Me-Ville is not marked out for us on a map. Jesus
is more virtual than tactile, like the avatar who faithfully reads and fre-
quently comments on our blog: We've never seen him/her, but we can't
deny that he/she exists.[13] The challenge for us is to look for small ways
of welcoming Jesus into our world and letting him look around. The
first step in following Jesus out of Me-Ville, then, is letting him in.

Many of my ongoing relationships are almost entirely virtual. I
interact with people as I post comments on their blogs and they post
comments on mine (www.loud-time.com). I post updates to my Facebook page and get updates in return from fellow Facebookers. The
Internet is our own virtual private universe, with its own doors and
locks.

I've noticed over time that my Internet persona is, while not entirely distinct from my in-person persona, definitely defined. I have a brand— slightly edgy, certainly sarcastic, generally silly but striving for profundity. I was admittedly discouraged to learn from a friend of mine that when run through some rating program, Loud Time had earned a G rating. Someone as edgy as I, with thoughts as sophisticated as mine, surely merits at least a PG rating, if not a PG-13.

The problem with cultivating an Internet persona so carefully is that sometimes people come knocking who know you too well to respect the boundaries of your personal brand. Comedian Jim Gaffigan has a routine in which two groups of friends finally meet, and he has to manage his persona in real time. He warns one group in advance: "They don't know I drink" and "Don't be surprised if I talk with a British accent."

We may not have gone to such extremes in how we present ourselves, but visitors confront our contrivances. I faced this dilemma most profoundly when my thirteen-year-old cousin friended me on Facebook. Now whoever viewed my profile would see among my friends an adolescent from the southern Midwest who loves redneck jokes and NASCAR events, whose own carefully cultivated persona involved not German theologians and underground music but professional bowling and white-boy hip-hop chic. He probably scored my coveted PG-13 rating without breaking a sweat. Behold, he stood at my virtual door and knocked. Would I let him in?

He's family, so of course I let him in. And he's been a good Facebook friend ever since.

Ultimately, when we strip away all the airs that we've put on, our true friends are those we are for and who are for us. When we understand that God is for us, when we realize that Jesus is pro-me, a knock at the door doesn't lose the sting of potential judgment and likely change, but it does lose the sting of an attack from the unfamiliar. We lead through the rooms of our refuge not an awkward stranger but the lover of our souls, who was present when we were formed in secret. We learn from Jesus where our public persona doesn't measure up with what he (and we) know to be true of ourselves. And he offers us a way into a life that is freer, truer.

The road to that life will be uncomfortable, however; for Jesus that road took him to the cross, and for us it means we'll be displaced from what we've been clinging to and exposed to the uncertainty of the road ahead.

• ESCAPE ROUTES •

RUTHLESS PERSONAL INVENTORY

In the last chapter we gave ourselves some time to assess how superbia sneaks into our interactions with other people. In this chapter we've considered what happens when Jesus sneaks in. It's time for a ruthless personal inventory, conducted alongside an all-powerful, perfectly pure God who, it just so fortunately happens, is pro-me.

Read the booklet *My Heart—Christ's Home* (mentioned in the chapter); then walk slowly through the rooms of your home, praying as you go. Estimate a rough breakdown of how much time you spend in each room over the course of a given week and what you find yourself doing there. Ask Jesus to give you insight into what those activities in that room are contributing to your spiritual health. Give particular attention to those temptations in your home that cultivate superbia—the centrality of your television, perhaps, and the cultural messages it conveys about entitlement and self-worth and perceived status; or the sites you frequent on the Internet from your computer and what you communicate about yourself by regularly visiting them; or the orientation and contents of your kitchen: the ratio of comfort food to staples of a nutritious diet and the amount of food and dishes in relation to the number of people you regularly invite over for a meal. You'll be tempted to treat yourself harshly during this exercise, but remember that Jesus is with you and that he's pro-you. He likes you and wants the best for you, and right now he wants you to know yourself more fully.

Give yourself a break for a while; then take a prayer walk through your

neighborhood and surrounding areas. Pray for your neighbors, asking yourself as you go what you know about them and what you *think* you know about
them based on the kind of unconscious assessments you observed yourself
making in chapter 1. What do you like about your neighbors and, more generally, your neighborhood? What gets in the way of a more meaningful
relationship between you and them? If Jesus is pro-you, what does it mean
for your neighborhood that he is also pro-them? In what sense is Jesus' love
for all of you enough common ground for overcoming barriers and becoming
truer neighbors to one another?[14]

Give yourself another break; then take a prayer drive through your community. What cultural messages do you observe as you go? In what ways are
the billboards, stores, and status symbols of your community reinforcing the
notion of entitlement? How do they promote self-absorption? What does your
community need to be delivered from? What tables in your community would
Jesus upend? What pharaohs would he confront with the message "Let my
people go"? Which of these would your community have the most trouble
leaving behind?

Keep in mind throughout these exercises that Jesus is *pro-me,* which
means that his intentions toward you, your neighborhood, and your community are all good. If you notice an air of superiority or righteous indignation
welling up in you as you walk or drive or pray, submit that feeling to Jesus,
asking him to help you be as *pro-me* as he is.

JESUS DISPLACES US

Sometimes the things you desire lead you astray. For me it was tacos. When I was in high school, I worked at a taco place—not one of those multinational microwaving meat-puppet taco places, mind you. My taco joint only dreamed of being multinational but had instead cast a relatively impressive regional shadow over my hometown and points west. We fried our own taco shells, refried our own beans, and seasoned and browned our own ground beef on-site. We bought our toppings fresh—never frozen—and we made each taco or burrito or plastic bin of nachos by hand. My hand, a fair bit of the time.

I went off to college, and bless my soul, two links in this regional fast-food chain were located there. I made excuses to grab a meal there every chance I could, and if I'd not met the taco maker before, I'd let him or her know that I too had once worn the apron and squirted the sour cream.

Meanwhile my parents moved across the country to a place that had not yet been graced by the regional taco chain's presence. My hometown era had ended, and once I graduated college and resettled in suburban Chicago, so had my ready access to the best burritos in the biz.

Until the summer of 2007, when my parents moved back to Iowa. I visited them in the new town soon after they arrived, and we celebrated my birthday with a tour of the city that culminated in the best tacos and faux-Mexican side items money could buy. I went back two weeks later for a family event and told myself that I would get there again, by hook or by crook.

The day got away from me, and by the time I had to leave, I was still tacoless. But I, confident in my innate tracking skills, wasn't concerned; I would find my own way there, by hook or by crook.

Forty minutes later I realized that I was (a) headed in the direction exactly opposite the location of the restaurant and (b) nowhere near any part of the state I had ever seen before. Eventually I got my bearings and got back on a recognizable road, but before I crossed the Mississippi River, I started to think, *I wonder if my taco franchise has made it to the Quad Cities?* I exited I-80 and by chance came across the precise restaurant I had lusted after, dreamed about, set out on my quest for. I ate my fill and got back into my car, at which point I quickly got myself lost once again.

This would never have happened to me in a place I call home, but when the thing we desire takes us out of the familiar and leads us into unknown territory, we suffer displacement.

Displacement isn't a bad thing; it's a necessary element of any journey. If we want to get anywhere we aren't, we can count on being displaced. The key is to plan for it. We can do some planning on our own—we can Google our destination and download driving directions; we can flip through our address book and figure out if anyone we know lives anywhere near where we're going. But the best plan for displacement is to trust ourselves to a trustworthy guide. A good guide already knows where we are, where we're headed, and what it will take to get from the one to the other.

WE CAN'T SAVE OURSELVES OR FULFILL OURSELVES

That's not our way, of course. The capacity of Americans to deny them-selves the benefits of an informed Other is the stuff of legend. It may have started at the gas station.

Once upon a time gas stations were called service stations. That means that when you pulled into the station, your only responsibility was to turn off the ignition. Waiting for you to wait on you was a serv-ice attendant who would bound up to your car, pop your gas cap, and commence pumping.[1]

While the gas flowed into your car, your service attendant would pop the hood and check your fluids. Assuming all was in order—which was likely, since the last time someone checked your oil was the last time you filled your tank, and since your car got six miles to the gallon, that wasn't that long ago, but since gas cost six cents a gallon, you didn't really care—the attendant would close the hood and clean your win-dows. Before long your tank was full, your fluids were topped off, your windows were clean, and you were on your way.

Unless you didn't know how to get where you were going, in which case the all-seeing, all-knowing service attendant was ready and willing to point you in the right direction. You just had to ask. And that's where the joke starts. "Why do men refuse to ask for directions?" Cue the laugh track.

This is Me-Ville, after all. To ask for directions is to admit weak-ness, to admit need. To receive help is to be in another's debt and, worse, to acknowledge that at least as it relates to geography, some-one else knows more than you. The temptation for the lost man is to figure it out in solitude, to assert all the more loudly and defiantly that he knows what he's doing, that he can get out of this jam he finds himself in, that despite appearances to the contrary, all is well in Me-Ville.

If the joke is going to work, it's not good for the man to be alone. He needs to be accompanied by the woman. If the temptation for the man is to deny his need, the temptation for the woman is to draw attention to it, to alert the man and any onlookers that while he doesn't have the sense to ask for help, she—not he—has what it takes to get them out of their sticky situation. So she leans over the man and asks the attendant, who bemusedly responds, "Oh, you're lost?"

Let me hasten to add, I don't consider this a genetic function of genders. No, this is social construct—superbians in competition with one another to establish, for themselves if for no one else, that the problem doesn't lie with them but with someone else: for the one, *If I were in charge, everything would be okay;* for the other, *We'd be fine if everyone would just leave me alone.*

The era of the full-service service station didn't last long. Wiper fluid and transmission fluid cost money, so the inclination of service stations to freely dispense said fluids waned over time. Gas costs money too, especially once oil-rich countries began working together to convert their natural resources into geopolitical power, so as costs rose, consumers demanded more fuel-efficient cars, and as fuel supplies dropped and long lines began to become the norm at filling stations, the idea of lounging around waiting for the tank to be filled lost its appeal. So consumers and suppliers reached the conclusion that everyone would be better off if they took care of their own cars, thank you very much. A happy side effect was that, with no attendant on hand to ask for directions, people could now get lost without the embarrassment of being found out.

Gas wasn't the only thing sending people into isolation. Around the same time, in the wake of the antiestablishment 1960s counterculture and numerous political scandals, public confidence in institutions such as the government, organized religion, and business corporations started to slip. John Lennon, recently divorced from his iconic band turned cultural monolith, the Beatles, recorded his now-famous diatribe "God":

> I don't believe in Jesus ...
> I don't believe in Elvis ...
> I don't believe in Zimmerman,
> I don't believe in Beatles ...
> I just believe in me.[2]

The heritage of this cultural sea change is paramount. Cable television allowed people to watch movies in the privacy of their homes rather than surrounded by others; pay-per-view and surround-sound home theaters simply enhanced the newly private experience and rewarded the impulse. People who once called "Information" to speak to an operator turned to Google to help themselves; operators returned the favor by ceding their craft to automated phone networks, so that anyone still inclined to ask a human being a question by phone was instructed by a recording to press one or two. Headphones transformed transistor radios from communal celebrations to private concerts, and iPods made each music consumer his or her own personal DJ. Snack food was repackaged out of group-friendly bags into cupholder-friendly tubes. All these innovations conspired to reinforce the central message that we're better off by ourselves, that we don't need each other. Those still foolish enough to admit need of one another found help harder and harder to come by. Whether you wanted to be or not, you were assimilated into the cultural idea *I am sufficient to myself.*

Self-sufficiency has to be taught, however, and the turn inward propagated by the culture isn't supported by the culture because we've been taught first and foremost to look out for number one and stay out of everyone else's business. So we're not just left alone; we're left to fend for ourselves. Some things are more achievable in isolation than others; I can check Wikipedia to get a rough idea of when and how to change the oil in my car, and from there I can, according to the spirit of the times, "fake it till I make it." But there are all kinds of life experiences and life choices for which a culture of self-sufficiency becomes not a privilege but a prison.

I once talked to a friend about a potentially life-changing decision my wife and I had to make, and make quickly. We were anxious; we had only some idea what the implications of that decision would be, how it would affect us, our family, our friends, our careers, our social life. To say yes to the question before us, we had determined, would change not only how we live our lives today but also very likely how we would spend our retirement. So yeah, we were anxious. And we were looking for a little outside advice.

I was nervous about discussing this decision out loud, however. It seemed so personally significant that to mention it to another person would change everything, leave me stripped bare, totally vulnerable. But my friend, I was convinced, would himself be directly affected by this decision—our friendship, how our families related to one another— so I thought I owed him a voice in the decision process. Besides, he's among the most commonsense people I know; he sees things much more clearly than I do. I didn't exactly ask him what I should do, but when you get down to it, that's exactly what I asked him.

His response was, "Wow, Dave, that's a really tough decision you have to make." Five minutes later he was back in his car, and I was once again alone with my thoughts, banished to the solitary center of my private universe.

I made the decision, of course, because I had to, but I learned in that moment that regardless of how competent we are to attend to the overwhelming events of our lives, regardless of how deep a hole we find ourselves in, ultimately in Me-Ville we will face such challenges alone.

JESUS TAKES HIS STAND

Good news, however. Jesus—that same Jesus who comes to visit us in Me-Ville and reveals to us where we've settled for a less-than-fulfilling life—makes a promise to us: "Never will I leave you; never will I forsake you" (Heb. 13:5 NIV). Leaving Me-Ville, however, is an entirely different proposition: Jesus didn't just come to visit; he came to get us. So be ready.

Jesus' first act in displacing us from Me-Ville is cognitive: We start to see our life through his eyes. While we're comforted by the fact that the invisible God has become present to us—we're assured that he's there—we're also subjected to his judgment. He looks at the things we've amassed for ourselves, the empire of relationships, achievements, and status we've built for ourselves, and asks us what good it all is. We feel ourselves judged by Jesus because we ourselves are learning to judge ourselves. It's a re-creation of the initial act of creation—Jesus honors us by helping us to name what we observe, calling it good or, more often perhaps, not good.

"You're right, Jesus; I *do* spend a lot of money on music and movies. I wonder why I do that."

"You're right, Jesus, for as long as I've known my neighbor, I really *don't* know all that much about her. I wonder why I haven't asked her about her life."

"You're right, Jesus. I *don't* treat my coworkers the way I want to be treated. I wonder why I haven't noticed that."

"You're right, Jesus. So much of my life *is* preprogrammed. I wonder why I don't stretch myself more."

"You're right, Jesus. Living in relative isolation here in Me-Ville *is* stifling, lonesome. I wonder what else is out there for me."

Jesus first and foremost offers us these kinds of epiphanies, but he is not content to stop there. Jesus' pro-me mission is not merely one of information but of *transformation*. As Dietrich Bonhoeffer, retelling the story of a rich young ruler being led through just such a life inventory by Jesus, puts it, "Jesus isn't concerned with the young man's problems, he's concerned with the young man himself."[3]

STOP BEING RICH, STOP BEING YOUNG, STOP BEING A RULER

In three gospels the story of the rich young ruler is prefaced by Jesus indulging little children and followed by Peter boasting of all that he and his peers have left behind to follow him. The theme throughout the passage is maturity in the face of transition. Jesus commands the rich young ruler—and Peter, and by extension, each of us—to stop being rich, stop being young, and stop being a ruler.

The ruler presumably has just seen Jesus show uncommon affection to the children of his community, and he suspects that this teacher might be able to address his aching sense that, despite his powerful position in the community, despite his religious fastidiousness, despite his enormous assets, all is not yet well for him. He is looking for Jesus to tell him what's left to accomplish: "Good teacher, what must I do to inherit eternal life?"

More likely he's looking for Jesus to say something like, "Are you kidding? You're fine—in fact, I wish these guys who keep following me

around were more like you." But whereas the little kids in the community needed to be assured that God loved them just as they were, Jesus
recognizes that the rich young ruler needs to be kicked out of a superbian nest.

So Jesus begins to deconstruct his life. First off, his faulty theology:
"Why do you call me good? Only God is good." Of course we know,
because we have the whole story, that Jesus is in fact good, because
Jesus is in fact God. But if it's a teacher this kid wants, it's a teacher he'll
get. "You know the commandments.... Do this and you shall live."
Jesus is guiding the rich young ruler into an important moment of
self-discovery: *All that I am (and I'm a lot) and all that I've done (and I've
done a lot) are not enough for all that I need.* The rich young ruler's life,
as good as it is, needs to change.

It's important to note that this kid—who has it all together—is no
less loved by Jesus than the little children he's just taken into his arms
and blessed, no less loved by him than the disciples who have already left
their comfortable lives behind. So Jesus gives him a gift. He moves from
a cognitive displacement to a behavioral displacement. "Go, sell all you
have, and give the money to the poor."

That's a tough break. Jesus has identified the guy's weak spot, something superbians judiciously protect. We protect that tender spot because
we recognize, at a heart level if not consciously, that Me-Ville is a prison.
And in prison you have to watch your back. Vulnerability is a liability in
Me-Ville, but vulnerability with Jesus, we learn, is our ticket out.

It's not enough, however, merely to realize that Me-Ville is a
prison. That's what nihilists do, and let's be honest, have you ever met
a happy nihilist? Nihilists have reached the conclusion, whether by
observing the world around them through the jaded lens of bitter experience or simply by reading people like Albert Camus and Jean-Paul

Sartre, that nothing means anything, that anything goes only because nothing matters. They've learned to think differently about the world they inhabit than many of us; what Jesus teaches us in intimate encounters such as this one with the rich young ruler, they've discovered in isolation. But because they're isolated in their discovery, they're left devoid of hope.

We don't just need to think differently if we want to break out of the prison that Me-Ville has become, for we learn from Jesus; we need to live differently. And Jesus says to the rich young ruler what he says to us: "Store up treasures in heaven"—get right with God, not with this faulty system you find yourself trapped in—"then come, follow me."

To attach yourself to a rabbi like Jesus is to admit that you have more to learn, that you're unable to teach yourself. Jesus is inviting the rich young ruler not just to grow up and redefine himself but to humble himself. The implicit promise from Jesus is that he will lift up this humbled young disciple to where he's not been before. A great adventure awaits.

The rich young ruler isn't ready, so he and Jesus part ways. In steps Peter, who's observed this interaction and apparently wants reassurance that Jesus is aware of all that his followers have already left behind. Jesus deftly turns Peter's comments around: Is Peter aware of all that lies in front of him? Are we?

Fortunately for Peter and for us, Jesus knows what lies beyond Me-Ville, and he doesn't just send us away; he invites us to follow him, to keep our eyes on him.

CHRIST THE CENTER

A lot of people use a nifty little illustration to describe how Jesus relates to us and helps us relate to God. It's called the Bridge Diagram—you

can draw it on a napkin, and anyone who can draw a stick figure is good
to go.

This is how it works. On the left side of the napkin you draw
you—or your hapless evangelistic victim—standing at the edge of a
deep cliff. I like to draw fire and alligators and stalagmites at the base
of the cliff just for dramatic effect because down there represents hell—
eternal torment in separation from God. Step two is to draw, on the
other side of the napkin, a stick-figure God standing on the edge of his
own cliff, eager to be in fellowship with you but separated by a chasm
full of your sinfulness. God is from Mars; you're from Venus. Or something like that.

What can bring you two together? Only the cross of Christ, which
when drawn correctly fits perfectly between the two cliff edges and creates a bridge for you to cross over. The net effect is that Jesus stands in
the gap between us and God; he's taken his rightful place in the center,
and we are fortunate for it.

As with any presentation of the gospel, this one has its limitations
of course, but it's a nice image—we begin as the center of the story,
but eventually that place is taken by Jesus, and we're happily relegated
to the periphery, where we can enjoy fellowship with God forever,
secure for eternity. That in itself is a nice corrective to our superbian
tendencies; John the Baptist readily embraced that place in the divine
story: "This is the assigned moment for him to move into the center,
while I slip off to the sidelines" (John 3:30).

Bonhoeffer extends the imagery of the Bridge Diagram, applying it
not only to our relationship with God but also to our relationships with
the other people we know, the institutions that exert influence over our
lives, and even ourselves.

A boundary which I am unable to cross … lies between
me and me, the old and the new "I." It is in the encounter
with this boundary that I shall be judged…. At this place
stands Christ, between me and me, the old and the new existence. Thus Christ is at one and the same time, my boundary
and my rediscovered centre.

In the fallen world the centre is also the boundary. Man
stands between law and fulfillment. He has the law, but he
cannot fulfil it. Now Christ stands where man has failed
before the law. Christ as the centre means that he is the fulfillment of the law. So he is in turn the boundary and judgement
of man, but also the beginning of his new existence, its centre.[4]

Between the law and its fulfillment, between us and God, between
us and each other, between our fear of God as Judge and our trust in
God as Deliverer, even ultimately between who we think we are and
who we were born to become—Jesus steps into that gulf because he is
for us enough to bear the weight that we can't bear ourselves. In so
doing, he displaces us to become the center of everything about us,
which is his rightful place.

JESUS IS HOMELESS AND INVITES US TO FOLLOW

Just because Jesus is centered doesn't mean Jesus is stuck, of course. Jesus
is on the move, and if he is to remain in the center, then we must adjust
our orbit accordingly. Jesus didn't merely say to the rich young ruler—
nor does he simply say to us—"You're wrong! Now straighten up!"
Having guided us in our epiphany of what is meaningless in our experience, Jesus then calls us onto a journey with him: "Come, follow me."

The rich young ruler "went away sad," disregarding Jesus' judgment and declining Jesus' invitation, "for he had great wealth." He wasn't alone, either. Lots of people refuse to follow Jesus out of Me-Ville. Many said straight up, "This is tough teaching, too tough to swallow," and gave up on him (John 6:60). I'm dubious about how I would have responded too; would I really voluntarily follow someone who's homeless, penniless, living off the largesse of other people, subjecting himself to the persecution of the powerful? How much of my worldview am I willing to forgo?

Look around as you go through the day today and ask yourself, *Would I ever give this up?* Not just things—what relationships would you be unwilling to set aside if, for whatever reason or even for no stated reason, Jesus walked up to you and said, "You need to let this one go"? What intangibles would you guard even from God—your professional reputation? Your impressive workout regimen? Your conspicuous social calendar? Your sense of personal security?

We do well to remember that Jesus gave up plenty not just on his way to the cross but, as Philippians 2 reminds us, on his way to the earth. By taking on flesh, Jesus lays aside the privileges of dwelling in unapproachable light. By making his ministry contingent on the faith of his hearers, Jesus forgoes the power available to him by divine right. By proclaiming the kingdom of God, Jesus subjects himself to the mockery and persecution of competing kingdoms. Jesus is already displaced when first we meet him, and he's inviting us into his displacement, which is undeniably an awkward invitation. "When Christ calls a man," Bonhoeffer puts it, "he bids him come and die."[5]

Many of Jesus' followers did, in fact, leave him, preferring the solitary sovereignty of the self they had grown accustomed to. But those who stayed—those who had recognized the emptiness of the experience

Jesus was delivering them from—began to see hints of the freedom he was delivering them to. They learned what the apostle Paul ultimately articulated: "If God is for us, who can be against us?" (Rom. 8:31 NIV). Jesus took his rightful place not only as center but also as the only Deliverer; we simply had to follow him to freedom.

> If Jesus is the Christ, the Word of God, then I am not primarily called to do the things that he does; I am met in his work as one who cannot possibly do the work he does. It is through his work that I recognize the gracious God. My sin is forgiven. I am no longer in death, but in life.[6]

Jesus takes his place in the center between
• God and us
• ourselves and everyone else
• the law that judges us and the fulfillment of the law that redeems us
• Me-Ville and the city of God
• the people we've been and the people God wants us to become
• death and life

PSALMS TO THE CENTER

With Jesus in the center, everything else starts to fall into its proper place. Keeping Christ in the center, however, is tough when we can't see him, and yielding our place at the center to him is tough when our problems seem so insurmountable, so unique to us. One way that has proved helpful to many is praying the Psalms.

I was drawn to the Psalms early on in my faith life, largely because so many of them were written by David, and he and I have the same name. But David did not write all of the psalms, which is immediately obvious: A single, solitary human being couldn't possibly embody such complexity of feeling in one life, right? In the Psalms we find people lashing out against God, people praying for their own death, people calling down violence against children. In the Psalms we find people bragging and whining and arguing and bargaining with God. We find all kinds of people being all kinds of people, and we find God in the center of their thoughts. Thomas Merton goes so far as to say that "the Psalms contain in themselves all the Old and New Testaments, the whole Mystery of Christ."[7]

That centrality of the Psalms has carried through the entire history of the Christian tradition. I was surprised one Sunday when an entire congregation sitting around me spontaneously recited from memory the Twenty-third Psalm, all the way from "The LORD is my shepherd" to "I will dwell in the house of the LORD forever." The Psalms have served as source material for songs of worship and self-expression all along; composer Anton Dvorak wrote a collection of such songs in 1894.

> The composer turned to the Bible against a personal background of grave and disturbing news.... A close friend and ardent devotee of Dvorak had died a month earlier in Cairo. And Dvorak's 80-year-old father lay gravely ill in distant Bohemia, where he died on March 26, two days after the last of the Biblical Songs was completed.
>
> Dvorak chose for these songs verses from the Czech version of the Book of Psalms (from Psalm 23 to Psalm 143),

gradually changing from expressions of despair (such as Nos. 1 and 8) and supplication (Nos. 2 and 3) to jubilation. The songs … go from an almost childlike faith to the feelings of despair, yet end on a note of rock-solid faith in God through Christ Jesus.[8]

The Psalms are so important to the faith that Jesus prayed them regularly. We hear him quote them in multiple discourses, applying even the most despairing thought—"My God, my God, why have you forsaken me?"—to himself (Ps. 22:1 NIV). When we read the Psalms knowing that Jesus prayed them earnestly in the same way that we sometimes find ourselves unwittingly praying them, we can take comfort in knowing that by ceding our place at the center to Jesus we aren't losing our voice: Jesus stands in solidarity with the worst of us, praying our prayers with us.

The psalms are so diverse that we sometimes can't relate to them. Some, perhaps, we may never relate to. This is important for our deliverance as well, because in discovering that not everything in the Bible relates to us we are reminded that we are not the center, that others have need of Jesus as well, that Jesus relates to them in ways that intimately connect to their souls' needs while still relating authentically and intimately to us. Jesus proves himself capable of holding it all together by being present to all of us at once.

We can also, by praying the Psalms, start to see our own troubles in their proper context. We struggle with the temptations and frustrations of life in Me-Ville not only alongside our contemporaries but with a great cloud of witnesses throughout history. What we're experiencing is nothing new. And yet what frustrates us, what tempts us, is verified as tempting and frustrating by the witness of history, by the witness of Christ. As Jesus displaces us and takes his proper place, we get the right perspective to truly understand who we are and what comes next.

What comes next is life after Me-Ville and the inevitable moments when we regret ever leaving and are tempted to return. We'll consider that impulse in the next chapter.

· ESCAPE ROUTES ·

PRAYING THE PSALMS

Pick a psalm, one that's familiar but not too familiar, and pray your way through it. Pay attention to your spirit as you go: Note which lines are particularly resonant with you, and which lines seem curiously irrelevant or downright troubling. I suggest beginning with Psalm 40.

The band U2 wrote a song based on the beginning stanza of Psalm 40 for its album *War* (calling the song, unimaginatively enough, "40") and for a decade or so ended each concert with it. People would walk to their cars still singing the chorus ("How long to sing this song?"). But the psalm continues well past where U2 left off.

Read through the psalm, considering the possibility that by doing so you're reading through someone else's prayer journal. Consider the intimacy of the relationship between the psalmist and the God he writes to; reflect on a similar moment of intimacy between you and God.

- What do you notice is still important to the psalmist about his life's circumstances even as he enjoys this moment of intimacy? In what ways is he inviting God into those circumstances?
- What circumstances in your life are creeping into your mind as you make your way through this psalm?
- Where can you see God entering into those circumstances? Does the thought of it give you joy? Hope? Resolve? Do you wonder if God's intervention will be enough?

Read through the psalm again, this time as your own prayer to God. End your time by reflecting on how the psalmist's last words make you feel about yourself and God:

And me? I'm a mess. I'm nothing and have nothing:
    make something of me.
You can do it; you've got what it takes—
    but God, don't put it off. (Ps. 40:17)

JESUS DELIVERS US

So now we're on the road. We've discovered that we've been living not in the best of all possible worlds, but in Me-Ville, where our self-absorption is not only slowly killing us personally but also setting up our whole world for a tragic collapse. We've discovered this by virtue of our new neighbor, Jesus, asking simple but telling questions of our patterns and quirks, leading us in the discovery that a better way of life is possible. We've learned that Jesus is for us, not against us, not ambivalent toward us. And so we've followed him out of Me-Ville and on the road to the kingdom he has in mind. We may have even started to get cute and referred to this coming kingdom as "Thee-Ville."

It's difficult to keep in mind in those first few steps of the journey God leads us on that the journey is not the destination and that we are far from free, far from safe, just yet. Journeys are regularly marked by an early exhilaration followed by a waning resolve to finish. We see it in stories such as *The Wizard of Oz*, where Dorothy and her friends start with a kick-step and a peppy, upbeat number, "We're Off to See the Wizard." Soon enough they're huddled together in fear of "lions and tigers and bears—oh my!" or they're tired of walking and contenting themselves to nap forever in a field of poisoned poppies.

We see it in stories such as *The Lord of the Rings,* where an initial reluctance to take the journey is replaced by excitement at the thought of journeying together, until eventually the gravity of the mission and the failings of the fellowship cause each one to harbor resentment against the others and a growing suspicion that they'd each be better off alone.

We see it even in the exodus of the Jews from Egypt en route to the Promised Land. In the early moments of their escape, they celebrate the victory of God over Pharaoh; they indulge in the treasures eagerly handed over to them by their former slave masters; they march with great energy out into the desert in pursuit of their God, who has promised them so much. But soon enough they are grumbling and complaining: Their feet hurt; they don't know where they're going or how long it's going to take; they don't have enough variety in their diet. Moses attempts on occasion to appeal to their sense of self-regard, if only to remind them not only of the kind of life on offer for them in a land of slavery but also of how special they should feel for bearing the privilege of being a chosen people, taken out of the status quo and set on a quest for the best life possible:

> Has any other people heard the voice of God speaking out of fire, as you have, and lived? Has any god ever tried to take for himself one nation out of another nation, by testings, by miraculous signs and wonders, by war, by a mighty hand and an outstretched arm, or by great and awesome deeds, like all the things the LORD your God did?
> (Deut. 4:33–34 NIV)

But for the most part, the people aren't buying it. Moses the liberator has morphed in the eyes of some—including his sister—into Moses the powermonger, Moses the buzzkill. The exodus has become the death march. The Promised Land starts to sound like a distant dream; the land of Israel's slavery sounds increasingly like a good place to raise a family.

The epic of any escape, including the escape from superbia, begins with displacement and its accompanying anxiety. Bonhoeffer in fact defined the early stages of discipleship, negatively, by its insecurity.

> The disciple is dragged out of his relative security into a
> life of absolute insecurity (that is, in truth, into the absolute
> security and safety of the fellowship of Jesus).[1]

We're safe here on the road; we just don't realize it yet. That's because we've become used to operating as we've been taught by the world. We need to be brought, in some cases dragged, into a new understanding of who we are and how we were meant to operate.

TAX-EXEMPT STATUS

By this time in our story, Peter had already embarked on his journey with Jesus. So in some sense Peter had already been delivered from Me-Ville, had already begun his new, redeemed life. His story, however, shows us how easy it is to turn back. One thing we're able quickly to ascertain about Peter is that he cares about what other people think of him. Peter acts off the cuff in grandiose, demonstrative acts, perhaps because he wants to get noticed, perhaps because he wants to be the first to do or say the right thing. It's endearing for the most part, but every once in a while such approval seeking gets him into trouble. Vulnerable as he was to the temptation to justify himself to the powers that be, for example, Peter was thrown off his game when he was confronted by religious leaders with the question of Jesus' adherence to the temple tax.

Odds are that Jesus, who had stormed through the temple disrupting the money changers there, was not overly concerned about paying this assessment, but Peter wanted to be right, to be the baseline for what passes for devout. So when the religious leaders suggested in front of Peter that Jesus wasn't doing what all good, faithful Jews ought to be doing, he denied it. He denied it because he's good at that sort of thing, and denying reality is an effective survival tactic when you're trapped alone in Me-Ville.

When Peter returned to Jesus' side, he learned the perplexing, scandalous truth—Jesus *didn't* believe in temple taxes. He had already confronted the Pharisees with the hard reality that even though the temple was nice and important, "one greater than the temple is now here." The presence of God in the covenant of Israel had relocated from the temple to Jesus, the incarnate Son of God. He, not some building, was the temple. The temple was no longer simply a pious ornament of Me-Ville; the temple was on the move.

That's a tough concept to grasp—the Pharisees didn't get it, and Peter's faith in Jesus was grounded more in experience than in dogma, so we may forgive him for being slow on the uptake. Jesus recognized this and gave him an object lesson: The temple tax would indeed be paid, for the sake of keeping things moving along, but not by Jesus nor by Peter—the temple tax would be paid by a fish.

"Go down to the lake, cast a hook, and pull in the first fish that bites. Open its mouth and you'll find a coin. Take it and give it to the tax men. It will be enough for both of us" (Matt. 17:27). Peter did what Jesus said, and it was so.

When Jesus displaces us, we're still faced with the temptations to fit in, to establish ourselves as okay, without defect. What we have to remember in those moments is that not only we, but whole systems that have been manufactured around us, have our origins in this discipline of self-assertion, of self-preservation. They're artifacts of the kingdom of self. As such, they are not okay; they're replete with defects. Meanwhile Jesus is doing his magic.

Peter is feeling insecure; that's okay, Jesus tells him. We'll continue to feel insecure while we abide in a world that has not entirely escaped its superbia. We'll continue to feel insecure when we're tempted to manufacture or shore up a reputation for ourselves or to adhere to some social standard being imposed on us. We'll continue to feel insecure for as long as we've taken steps out of Me-Ville but still have it in our sights.

Meanwhile Jesus has accommodated Peter's insecurities without sabotaging Peter's growing faith. The means by which Peter would be able to shore up his self-esteem would be undeniably miraculous. This wasn't some benefactor paying his bills on his behalf; this wasn't Peter not quitting his day job; this was the one fish in the Sea of Galilee with a four-drachma coin in its mouth deciding it would take Peter's bait— and Jesus knowing about it in advance. Me-Ville was still there, and Me-Ville still made claims on Jesus' followers, but they were no longer inextricably beholden to it.

SUPERBIAN SPIRITUALITY

We have temple taxes in our own day. We reject the world and embrace the kingdom of God and then learn to express our devotion to God in particular ways—some of us by regular church attendance, some of us by serving in multiple ministries of our churches, some of us by setting aside devotional time every day, some of us by setting all our radio pre-sets to Christian music or Christian talk stations, some of us by all the above. We learn these methods from those who have gone before us, and we put them into practice religiously. And then, when we see some-one else doing something different, we're troubled. *Why aren't they doing what I'm doing? What's wrong with them? Surely nothing's wrong with me!*

I went to a Christmas party with my wife once where each person was instructed to bring a book that had been meaningful in his or her experience of the Christian life, to be received as a gift by someone else at the table. I freely admit I was showing off when I wrapped up a large commentary on the book of Genesis, peppered with quotations from the ancient church fathers, representing the best theological thinking about Genesis from the first eight centuries of Christian history. Truth be told, I'm showing off right now just by bringing it up. But I digress. I dutifully wrapped up the commentary and put it in the center of the table, envious of the unsuspecting tablemate who would soon have his or her faith rocked by this early Christmas present.

Eight books covered in wrapping paper sat in the center of our table throughout the meal. Mine was the biggest. Finally we reached the point in the evening where we each would blindly select a book. A woman grabbed mine—*She must be really greedy, grabbing the big one before any-one else could get to it,* I thought—unwrapped it, sighed, and promptly handed the commentary to her husband.

I was livid; this woman had no idea what she was giving up; she didn't deserve to have the book in her home. If my book was a pearl, then she was a pig. I wanted to grab the book back from her husband and storm out. But I hadn't opened my gift yet.

I went last because I'm not greedy like some people. I picked up the teeny-weeny little present lying alone amid the torn wrapping paper at the center of the table and unwrapped it. I held in my hands the latest high-profile, high-concept, lowbrow waste of paper I'd read about in recent book reviews. Clearly someone hadn't read the instructions; this wasn't a deep soul-moving book—this was pablum in print. The card justified its inclusion among the other books not because the person had been caught up to the second heaven while reading it or because its contents had launched a great awakening somewhere; the giver had justified the book with the vague, noncommittal endorsement "It encourages spiritual growth."

I was livid; I wanted to throw that book across the room; I wanted to burn it under the heat lamps at the buffet table. Instead I smiled and said thank you and nudged my wife under the table that it was high time we left.

Our devotion to God doesn't inoculate us against superbia. In fact, in some ways, it aggravates it, in the sense that we elevate markers of spiritual progression over moments of spiritual profundity. Brian Mahan identifies the temptation to use "religious language, the language of the Christian narrative—its sacred stories, historical traditions, and espoused values—to hide from themselves and others the power that some of their hidden desires exercise over their lives."[2] Without regular reminders that we do all things incompletely in our own strength, we fall easily back into an arrogance that not only lends itself to judgment but also predisposes us to anxiety. Bonhoeffer puts it this way: "I can lay on a very nice show for myself even in the privacy of my own room. That is the extent to which we can distort the word of Jesus."[3] A passage in the little book *Quiet Time* betrays this vulnerability in how we, bound to particular cultures, understand ourselves in relation to others by how we relate personally to God.

There is a passion for Christ which it has been given to very few to possess, but which has set those who have it apart for ever from their fellow men. Is not this the quality which separates between Christian and Christian, which marks out some—the rare ones—as beings apart from the rest of us?[4]

If you're raised with a particular understanding of what's foundational to a relationship with God, you will be inclined to see yourself among those "very few" who have been "set … apart for ever from their fellow men." You'll be inclined to see yourself as a better Christian even than other members of your church, who deign to call themselves "Christian" but fail to make a strong commitment (or as strong a commitment as you) to a daily "quiet time" or monthly retreat or some other spiritual discipline. You will feel an inordinate pressure to be one of "the rare ones," and when you fall short, your world will be shaken.

This drive to serve as the baseline for holiness is caught up in the tension between our need to belong and our need to distinguish ourselves from one another. Jean Vanier writes that

There is an innate need in our hearts to identify with a group, both for protection and for security, to discover and affirm our identity, and to use the group to prove our worthiness and goodness, indeed, even to prove that we are better than others.… If it were not religion or culture that people used as a stick with which to beat others, they would just use something else.[5]

The truth is, Jesus reveals to us over time that our devotional life is a matter between us and him, not us and us or even me and myself. So profound a spiritual giant as the monk Thomas Merton puts our devotional life in its proper place in a single sentence: "It is not important to live for contemplation, but for God."[6] So whether we're judging ourselves against the practices of others or judging others by how we operate, we are displacing Jesus from the center and replacing him with someone or something that can't bear the weight and hasn't earned the spot. The people at my table at the Christmas party were by and large as interested in their own spiritual development as I was in mine, but they are different people from me, and so they will draw near to God in different ways than I would. I had been given an opportunity to share myself with some other people, and I had taken instead the opportunity to elevate myself at their expense. I had turned a gift into a test and declared myself the standard against which everyone else would be graded.

We do have ways of encouraging one another to follow Jesus and to be in right relationship with God, and it's appropriate to suggest ways they might go about doing that, but in the moment I attempt to indoctrinate someone else into a system for which my only frame of reference is my personal experience, I have begun to organize my own cult. I might as well file for tax-exempt status.

That's what the Pharisees tried to do with Peter and the temple tax and, by extension, with Jesus. But Jesus wasn't having it. And he still wasn't having it after his resurrection when he told Peter what his future would be like and Peter looked over at John and asked, "What about him?"

Jesus' response was telling: "If I want him to live until I return, what is that to you? You, follow me." This started rumors, of course, that John would live forever. But only because Jesus' followers still had one foot in Me-Ville. Jesus was in all likelihood merely making a ludicrous claim to prove a point: To the extent we compare ourselves to one another, we are still trapped in the life God is calling us out of.[7] Despite our conscious and unconscious attempts to put ourselves, or occasionally other people, in the center, Jesus confronts us with the reality that he has never given up the center, and he displaces us all over again.

We of course do have responsibility to one another, and our journey out of Me-Ville will consider that in a later chapter, but for now we can return to Bonhoeffer, who in centering Christ placed him between each of us and everyone else.

> Without Christ there is discord between God and man and between man and man. Christ became the Mediator and made peace with God and among men. Without Christ we should not know God, we could not call upon Him, nor come to Him. But without Christ we also would not know our brother, nor could we come to him. The way is blocked by our own ego.... Only in Christ are we one, only through him are we bound together. To eternity he remains the one Mediator.[8]

Our interactions without Christ at the center are fundamentally flawed and get us into trouble; seeing people by way of Christ allows us to extend grace when we encounter their flaws and allows Christ to protect them from the flaws we bring to the encounter. Dallas Willard put it this way:

> Among those who live as Jesus' apprentices there are no relationships that omit the presence and action of Jesus. We never go "one on one"; all relationships are mediated

through him. I never think simply of what I am going to do
with you, to you, or for you. I think of what we, Jesus and
I, are going to do with you, to you, and for you. Likewise, I
never think of what you are going to do with me, to me, and
for me, but of what will be done by you and Jesus.[9]

With Christ at the center we see ourselves and one another where
we all ought to be: in his orbit.

SELF-EFFACEMENT AND THE KNOWLEDGE OF GOD

Meanwhile, having been brought by Jesus out of Me-Ville, we have a
better view of its impact on us. Look at the Sermon on the Mount in
Matthew 5—7, where Jesus makes the paradoxical statements "So let
your light shine before others" and "Don't call attention to yourself."
Bonhoeffer hints at this paradox, that in being liberated from our self-
absorption we actually get a fuller understanding of ourselves.

There is a pointed contrast between [Matthew] 5 and 6.
That which is visible must also be hidden.... We are to hide
it from *ourselves*. Our task is simply to keep on following,
looking only to our Leader who goes on before, taking no
notice of ourselves or of what we are doing. We must be
unaware of our own righteousness, and see it only in so far
as we look unto Jesus; then it will seem not extraordinary,
but quite ordinary and natural. Thus we hide the visible
from ourselves in obedience to the word of Jesus.... If you
do good, you must not let your left hand know what your
right hand is doing, you must be quite unconscious of it.

Otherwise you are simply displaying your own virtue, and
not that which has its source in Jesus Christ. Christ's virtue,
the virtue of discipleship, can only be accomplished so long
as you are entirely unconscious of what you are doing.[10]

He goes on to call it imperative "for the Christian to achieve renun-
ciation, to practise self-effacement, to distinguish his life from the life
of the world."[11]

Self-effacement is a scary notion; we read it as self-extinction
and we envision supposedly pious practices like starving ourselves and
wearing hair shirts. We have church history to thank for that:
Extreme ascetic practices among the desert fathers of the ancient
church and wild-eyed expressions of devotion from medieval mystics
have been officially saluted and thus have defined the practice for us
and segregated it into some substrata of the "super-devout." In giving these hyper-devoted disciples special status, we've also excused
ourselves from the very practical kind of self-effacement Jesus is calling us to in the Beatitudes:

> You're blessed when you're at the end of your rope....
> You're blessed when you feel you've lost what is most dear
> to you....
> You're blessed when you're content with just who you
> are—no more, no less....
> You're blessed when you've worked up a good appetite
> for God....
> You're blessed when you care....
> You're blessed when you get your inside world—your
> mind and heart—put right....

You're blessed when you can show people how to cooper-
ate instead of compete or fight....

You're blessed when your commitment to God provokes
persecution. (Matt. 5:3–10)

Taken at their most simple, the Beatitudes are a progression: a
point of realization that leads us to relinquishment that turns us
toward God and refashions our understanding of the world around
us, to the point where the world around us is threatened by our simply being our new selves. These are not status-seeking disciplines so
much as they are the outward impact of a very personal, intimate
reckoning with God. God isn't establishing us as some special cate-
gory of super-Christian here; he's simply leading us out of Me-Ville,
and the world is alternately enticed and threatened simply by watching us go.

Think of how much better you know yourself when you're at the
end of your rope: You have a sense of not only what you've lost but also
what it's meant to you. Your sense of loss quite intuitively leads to a radical inventory of where your life has led you and what you have to show
for it. And to move from there to contentment—that's the joy of the
recovering addict, to breathe fresh air after choking for years breath after
toxic breath. And to see your appetite redirected is to be virtually born
again, to find yourself looking at a wholly different world. And to then
fully feel your affections toward this new world that in reality is not all
that different from your old world is like receiving a brand-new call, a
new responsibility, one you can fully embrace even when it irritates people that you've done so, even when it becomes immediately obvious that
your calling will occasionally irritate you because it involves people who
are occasionally irritating.

The slaves who were delivered out of Egypt by Moses had precisely this kind of journey:

- At the end of their rope in Egypt, they cried out to God.
- Displaced from their four-hundred-year home, their deliverance involves an unsettling good-bye.
- Wandering in the desert they come to understand themselves without the constraints and trappings of the culture they've left.
- Presented with the law by a God who has miraculously provided for them, they begin to crave righteousness.
- Permanently removed from the dehumanizing status of slaves, they begin to relate to one another with dignity and compassion.
- Forced to choose between a life with or without God, they choose life.
- Presented with the complications of living as a community, they learn to live well together.
- Emboldened by God's power and faithfulness, they endure the challenges of new enemies.[12]

Thomas Merton makes that same journey through the cross but keeps its intensely intimate nature in view:

> The right kind of withdrawal ... has taught me how to live. And now I owe everyone else in the world a share in that life. My first duty is ... to live as a member of a human race which is no more (and no less) ridiculous than myself. And my first human act is the recognition of how much I owe everybody else.[13]

FORGETTING OURSELVES ON PURPOSE

This is the primal, organic experience of self-effacement that we've lost sight of over centuries of institutional Christianity. I, let me quickly add, have no issue with institutional Christianity; it's perfectly sensible for a growing group of people gathered around a common cause to attempt to organize itself and to come up with ways of managing people's expectations of it. To do so involves keeping peoples' eyes on the prize, so to speak: to get everyone to agree on what is most noble and true about what's been done in the institution's name and to provide some kind of context for the things that are apparently noble but frustratingly extreme along the way. We need a way to make sense of the hair-shirt-wearing, dung-eating, wild-eyed prophets who carried the cross as they went before us.

We've taken most often to calling them saints, but in the process we've lost sight of the fact that for the most part they weren't trying to be saints; they were trying to be themselves—making their way as honestly as possible through the process that God was intimately guiding them on, from the end of their rope to the "recognition of how much" they owe God and the world. That's how Thomas Merton ultimately, begrudgingly, came to interpret sainthood: "For me to be a saint means to be myself.... Therefore the problem of sanctity and salvation is in fact the problem of finding out who I am and discovering my true self."[14]

Ethicist Brian Mahan, in his book *Forgetting Ourselves on Purpose,* sees this process as the responsible practice of ambition. It's sensible for us to want what's good for ourselves, and it's sensible to pursue what's good for ourselves. Along the way, however, we need to be intellectually honest with ourselves.

We do whatever it takes to avoid admitting that our
ambitions come to us already scripted, complete with
instruction manual. We think of ambition as a kind of
dynamic power or force field. Ambition is simply "the fuel of
achievement," and what direction we take and what our destination may be are entirely up to us. If we desire fame, wealth,
and power, well, that's what we desire. But others have ambition for world peace and inner harmony, and that's all right
too. Ambition is whatever we make of it.

But this is nonsense. It is closer to the truth to say that
we are what our ambitions make of us.... In American society, in part because of our accent on egalitarianism and our
antipathy toward inherited class structure, individual achievement is supremely important. In itself, this is neither good
nor bad. It is merely part of the script. The trouble is that it
becomes difficult to assess achievement and monitor happi-
ness without surrendering to the impulse to adopt invidious
comparison as a prime measure of individual worth.[15]

Christianity is like everything else in that over time its scripts have
been written and memorized without our even being conscious of it.[16]
We're conscious, instead, of one another; and because we've inherited
not only the scripts of our religion but also the scripts of our culture,
we look for ways of distinguishing ourselves from one another, of being
"holier than thou" or "more relevant than thee"—whatever we're more
capable of pulling off. Bonhoeffer's paradox, like all good paradoxes,
challenges these subconscious scripts: We are called to live in a way
that others will emulate without seeking a platform for ourselves to
display our greatness; we ought to strive to be our best selves without

obstructing others' pursuit of God's calling on their lives; we must somehow, to paraphrase Jesus, ensure that the left hand is doing good without letting the right hand know what it's doing.

We might call the task of our left hand the particular vocation that Jesus has called us individually to and the task of our right hand the self-effacement that Jesus calls all of us generally to. Mahan calls ambition the "raw material of vocation," and so the challenge we're faced with is to discover how the raw material of our ambitions can be refined and processed so that it serves our vocation without polluting our presence in the world.[17]

AGERE CONTRA

One way some Christians have sought, to good effect, to put this left-hand/right-hand paradox into practice is through the Jesuit notion of *agere contra*, which is Latin for "act against."[18] The notion behind *agere contra* begins with the assumption that we naturally gravitate toward those people, places, things, and experiences that are most comfortable to us. This is a good, sensible developmental practice, helping people to form a basic, unconscious way of making sense of the world. We might revisit Eden to understand this foundational value: Adam is bewildered by the whirlwind naming of all of creation, at the end of which his most profound sense was that none of what God made was quite like him, that he was ultimately alone, that out of all this good world something was not quite good. Then he fell asleep, and when he woke up, there was Eve—bone of his bone, flesh of his flesh—and all was good in the world again. You might say that Adam and Eve naively gravitated toward one another because they were like one another, which was God's design and intent. They needed each other to provide them with a baseline, some stability at the foundation that would help them to rightly order and ultimately make sense of the wildly diverse world they'd inherited.

Those people, places, things, and experiences that establish our baseline for us thus become our teachers, our directors, feeding us lines from our scripts and helping us find our places on the stage we've entered. Eventually, however, the production we're a part of suffers for the conspicuousness of the direction we're getting. The challenge discerned by the Jesuits, at this point, is to "press against" the norms that we've established for ourselves and stretch ourselves into not what we think we ought to be or what we want to be perceived as being but who God is truly intending us to be.

I was in a play recently where up until the dress rehearsal none of the actors was "off script," delivering our lines without outside help. Some of us were carrying our scripts around, flipping pages furiously till we found the next word of our monologue; others of us punctuated each thought with the word "Line!" which cued the assistant director to tell us what we were supposed to say next. Our director wisely determined that our audience would not be entertained by the assistant director's loud offstage whispers, so she cut us off: no scripts in hand, no lines fed to us by her assistant. We were now officially "off script," whether we wanted to be or not. We would live or die by what came out of our mouths, not what was written for us or fed to us.

To add to the pressure, this play was a performance of the gospel of John, the very Word of God. Improvising lines would be not only unentertaining, but it ran the risk of being downright heretical.

What we discovered in that dress rehearsal, however, was that we knew our parts better than we thought we did. We had become addicted to the comfort of the script and the ready presence of our assistant director; we had lazily accepted help that for the most part we didn't need. With our hands free of our scripts, and with our minds focused not on the lines but on the scene, we were able to more freely and truly act, and we delivered our lines more sensitively and compellingly.

That's the principle behind *agere contra*. James Martin puts it this way:

> If there is a part of ourselves that is not free, we try to "act against" that part in order to free ourselves from resistance in that area … so as to invite [ourselves] into the experience of finding God in that unexpected place and move past [our] fear. All of this is a way to grow in freedom and love.[19]

We reach a point in our development when it's no longer appropriate for us to rely on the scripts we've been given; it becomes time for us to push against the comfortable points in our life and stretch into new territory.

God knows that what we are at any given moment is only at best a foreshadowing of what we're becoming. He knows that we're always vulnerable to a sense of superbia that allows us to think that wherever we've come to rest our head at any given moment simply must be where we were meant forever to be. In those moments we need to be rescued from ourselves, delivered from our self-constructed prisons. So God tells Abraham, who is perfectly content living in Haran, "Leave this place [which you know] and go to the land I will show you [which you don't know]." He tells Moses to pack up the people of Israel and leave Egypt to go to some undisclosed land flowing with milk and honey. He tells the prophet Jeremiah to lie on his side naked for a month, cooking his food over animal waste, rather than simply sending the king a letter telling him not to commit idolatry. God even goes so far as to leave the comfort of heaven himself, taking on flesh with all its limitations; enduring a life of obscurity, poverty, and relative powerlessness; facing the mockery and persecution of the powers that be; and subjecting himself to a cruel and vicious death that provides the ultimate deliverance from the self-destruction that we've each and all consigned ourselves to. Jesus, our Savior and Lord, embodies *agere contra* supremely from the beginning of his ministry to its end.

The common denominator of all these God-initiated radical acts, believe it or not, is grace. Jesus lived, suffered, and died as an act of grace. But God's call to us to live outside our comfort zone is likewise an act of grace, because such calls are systematically severing the ties that bind us to Me-Ville. Vanier recognizes that Jesus, the Truth, calls us into uncomfortable truth because he loves us and wants what's best for us:

> We need to strive to live in truth, because the truth sets us free, even if it means living in loneliness and anguish at certain moments…. The truth will set us free only if we let it penetrate our hearts and rend the veil that separates head from heart. It is important not only to join the head and the heart, but to love truth, also, and to let it inspire our lives, our attitudes, and our way of living.[20]

This pursuit of the truth about ourselves necessarily involves an openness to others. The thing about *agere contra* is that you can't effectively practice it in isolation. It's too easy to forgive ourselves for not really separating from the comforts that enslave us, and too many influences surround us that tempt us back toward our comforts. It's funny: As I write this section, my computer keeps automatically changing the word *agere* to the word *agree*, as though the entire notion of *agere contra* is absurd, as though I couldn't possibly want to make myself uncomfortable, as though I surely mean to conform to some preestablished vocabulary rather than write something distinct. In a similar way we are regularly being subtly indoctrinated into the status quo that surrounds us—whether that status quo is social or religious or some hybrid of the two. Because this pull is so insidious, we need help identifying it.

We also need help guarding ourselves against the kind of self-satisfaction that can accompany a spiritual discipline such as *agere contra*. Merton recognizes this pious temptation:

> When a proud man thinks he is humble his case is hopeless.
>
> Here is a man who has done many things that were hard for his flesh to accept.... It is reasonable that his conscience should be at peace. But before he realizes it, the clean peace of a will united to God becomes the complacency of a will that loves its own excellence.... He burns with self-admiration and thinks: "It is the fire of the love of God."
>
> He thinks his own pride is the Holy Ghost.[21]

Some of Jesus' most biting, confrontational words were directed not at people who were far removed from the community of faith but at the people who led such communities. In one instance Jesus healed the sight of a man born blind, whose blindness had been interpreted by religious Jews as some deep-seated sin in his family. Jesus' parting shot at those Pharisees was telling: "Those who have made a great pretense of seeing will be exposed as blind.... Since you claim to see everything so well, you're accountable for every fault and failure" (John 9:39–41).

I think Jesus confronted people of faith because it's so easy to settle into a religion that serves as a crutch. We're not typically even aware of the ways we do this, so we laugh when outside observers—atheists and agnostics, skeptics and cynics—accuse us of that very thing. But then there's Jesus, accusing people of faith of treating religion as a crutch.

Religion is, in fact, a pretty tempting crutch when you've been untethered from the props of superbia. Outside observers of Christian faith—people whose primary residence is still in Me-Ville—are not surprisingly unconscious of the various institutions and practices that serve as crutches for them. But upon leaving Me-Ville, you no longer have ready access to such props. Meanwhile you've entered into a culture within the larger culture, and you're tempted to use that culture in the way all manufactured cultures get used: to support the self, to prop up your ego, to indulge your self-regard.

So our churches need to be on constant watch against such commodification. The simplest way to do that is to invite Jesus to church.

That sounds cheeky, I know, and I suppose it's meant to be. But there are two other more common ways of going to church: The first is to go in search of Jesus; the second is to go as an impartial consultant. Either way, our approach is missing something—or more appropriately, someone.

To go to church in search of Jesus is to put inordinate pressure on church to be perfect, to fulfill all our dreams about what heaven must be like and what our private universe should begin to resemble. In church, for example, everyone is always honest and always loving, always patient and never petty, always happy and never sad. Church is all these things because that's where God lives, because that's where Jesus is. Such naivete will satisfy us for a while until we discover that someone's been less than loving or less than honest with us, when someone isn't patient with us or we find ourselves unsettlingly petty with someone else, when someone is so sad that we don't know what to do with them or ourselves. A simple trip to church on that day becomes a crisis of faith.

On the flip side, occasionally we go to church with our arms crossed, a crusader against superficiality in religion. We deconstruct the worship team and pick apart the sermon. We look for pettiness to confront and crass materialism to overturn. We live out our inner consultant, so to speak—all critique with no long-term investment to the community we're critiquing.

Both such approaches to church are responses to legitimate concerns. We want the church we attend to be culturally significant and faithful to its Christian heritage. We want the people who occupy our church to be growing spiritually without being cloistered from the curious. We want all these paradoxical things for our church. And in reality, so does Jesus.

The difference is that Jesus is able to be consistently, persistently *pro-me* in his attitude toward his church, and we're not. So when we neglect to tether ourselves to Jesus before we darken the doors of our church, we open ourselves to the possibility of being, in the words of Dietrich Bonhoeffer, "a destroyer of the brethren."

The best church is one where people are led to one another by Jesus. We each need people who have come from where we've come from: who are refugees like us from Me-Ville en route to the city of God that Jesus is guiding us toward. In such a church we come to count on one another without making idols of one another, because Jesus is still in view, out in front. We're the kind of collection of friends who don't sit around face-to-face, so absorbed with one another that they're blind to all other influences; rather they stand side by side, pointed toward Jesus, who's taking them on a journey.[22]

As we become accustomed to this collection that Jesus has gathered us into, we become more like a family on a road trip than a bunch of solitary commuters on a train. We get to know one another, and we discover that we're for one another—not in a way that idolizes the other but in a way that actually loves one another, bearing one another's burdens and encouraging one another onward. We're surrounded by people who know us well enough to know what we need to press against and who will recognize when we've slipped into idolatry, thinking that the way we're combating our weaknesses is actually a marker of our superiority.

God fills this role with himself, of course, through the witness of Scripture, which shows us how far short we fall of his glory, and through the presence of the Holy Spirit, who convicts us of our fallenness, and through the person of Jesus, whose example and ministry show us to be people who need God. But he also fills this role for each of us with one another, surrounding us with people who know us too well to put up with our vanity and who love us too much to let us be less than we ought. The community that God is building among us as he leads us from Me-Ville to Thee-Ville is the subject of the next chapter.

(• ESCAPE ROUTES •)

TAKE JESUS TO CHURCH

Before you leave for church—whether a worship service or a bake sale or a committee meeting or, if your church is a group of people who all live together, your living room—ask Jesus to stand between you and everybody else. Observe the event not as a generic visitor or as a semiconscious attendee or even as a worshipper in the throes of spiritual passion; observe the event through the eyes of Jesus, who died for this church but holds authority over it as its Lord. Be prepared to confront the church where you perceive it falling short of what Jesus expects of it, but be prepared to do so quietly, cautiously, respectfully. Be prepared also to note where the church or its people need love and grace and mercy, and then act on that impulse.

Then go home and journal your experience. Ask God to give you insight into questions such as the following:

- What did I see today that I am more interested in preserving than Jesus would be?
- What did I see today that I am more frustrated by than Jesus would be?
- Where was I tempted to lead more aggressively than Jesus would?
- Where was I tempted to let pass what Jesus would confront?
- Who needed to experience the love of God today and didn't? Why not?

5

JESUS BINDS US TOGETHER

Read the gospel of John closely enough, and you see hints of a long-standing rivalry between Peter, the rock on which Jesus built his church (Matt. 16:17–19), and John, the disciple Jesus loved dearly (John 13:23). Whereas Matthew and Mark suggest that Peter was the first to call Jesus the Messiah, John's gospel glosses over Peter's profession and, even more so, Jesus' response that pegged Peter as de facto leader of the church. To hear John tell it, Peter (known then as simply Simon) seems to be the last one to figure it out. In John's gospel Peter virtually stumbles onto Jesus, knuckles dragging on the ground behind him, by way of his brother Andrew (who introduces Jesus as the Messiah). Before Simon can even grunt, Jesus gives him the nickname Peter, or Rock, seemingly out of the blue, providing no rationale whatsoever. Peter is actually the only disciple in this story that doesn't declare Jesus as Messiah (John 1:40–42).

By the end of the gospel of John, Peter has made a fool of himself as Jesus attempts to wash his feet, has cut the ear off an innocent servant against Jesus' orders, has denied his relationship with Jesus three times, has dived into a lake like an idiot chasing after Jesus while the other disciples tended responsibly to his boat. No walking on water for Peter in

John's gospel; John even suggests that Jesus liked him better (his head was reclined on Jesus' shoulder during the Last Supper) and that Peter couldn't keep up with him in a footrace (John 20:4, 8).

It's important to keep in mind that the Gospels were not diaries kept by the disciples as a day-by-day accounting of Jesus' activities and sayings. They were memoirs written years, even decades, after the fact, firsthand accounts of the person a generation of people had come to believe was the Son of God and Deliverer of the human race. So John wasn't dissing Peter in the moment only to later apologize and recant; John was making it a matter of historical record, for millennia to come until Jesus comes again, that he's faster than Peter and that Jesus always liked him best.[1]

Ladies and gentlemen, meet the founders of our faith. In this corner, the first human head of the Christian church; in that corner, the disciple of love, who outlived all the others. Let the petty party begin.

I find it oddly reassuring to know that even those closest to Jesus, those whose leadership and writings came to define the Christian church, had these foibles to their character. It takes some of the pressure off. That the person who wrote, "Let us love one another, for love comes from God" (1 John 4:7 NIV), was nevertheless vulnerable to the petty jealousies and insecurities that plague each of us from day to day removes some of the sentimental idealism of the notion that because God loved us, so we love one another (John 13:34–35).

Nevertheless, it's significant that Jesus, knowing the tension that would persist between these two disciples, and surely other disciples he called, and undoubtedly disciples down through the ages, nonetheless persistently subjected them to one another. We don't see Jesus send Peter in one direction and John in another; we don't see him giving Peter one set of instructions and John another. We do see him gather them and us together and say directly, "Let me give you a new command: Love one another" (John 13:34).

The challenge that John and Peter faced in that verse is the same challenge that faces us. We realize soon enough upon our departure from Me-Ville that more than one set of footprints track through the sand; Jesus is not plucking us individually out of trouble but gathering together a people for himself, establishing a kingdom that will reign forever, and teaching us how to inhabit that kingdom as a community of faith.

EVERY CHRISTIAN IS BOUND TO EVERY OTHER

Peter, our tour guide from Me-Ville to Thee-Ville, writes this to those people who, in the years following Jesus' resurrection and ascension to heaven, gave themselves to him and took up the journey of discipleship:

> You are a chosen people, a royal priesthood, a holy
> nation, a people belonging to God, that you may declare the
> praises of him who called you out of darkness into his won-
> derful light. Once you were not a people, but now you are
> the people of God. (1 Peter 2:9–10 NIV)

This is an ennobling portrait reminding us, after we've perhaps spent a fair bit of time recognizing how finite, fickle, and fallen we are, that God really does like us, really does want to be with us forever. It's also a subtle reminder that we're not alone, that God isn't simply inviting us into a private perpetual conversation. Bonhoeffer puts it this way: "The same Mediator who makes us individuals is also the founder of a new fellowship."[2] I, an individual, am chosen by God as part of a

118

DELIVER US FROM ME-VILLE

people, ordained by God as part of a royal priesthood, consecrated by God as part of a nation. This is a marked contrast to the kingdom we've left, where every home is some person's castle, walled off from one another. In Me-Ville we could hardly be called a people, but outside its walls, en route to the kingdom of God, we find ourselves collected into the people of God.

Peter earlier makes this notion literally more concrete, as he switches the imagery back and forth from us as human beings to us as rocks— that same nickname Peter himself had been given by God years previously: "You also, like living stones, are being built into a spiritual house to be a holy priesthood" (1 Peter 2:5 NIV). In this sense we are enmeshed with one another, mortared together so that we can't consider ourselves outside the context of each other. Regardless of how Peter and John feel about each other, they are being bound together by Jesus. Regardless of how you and I feel about each other, we are being bound together by Jesus.

This is either a profound contrast to, or an unsettling fulfillment of, Jean-Paul Sartre's cheeky statement: "Hell is other people." To be frank, it depends on the day.

I happen to work for a company that is organized around a statement of faith; employees must affirm that statement of faith year in and year out. That means that for forty-plus hours a week, every week, I'm surrounded by people who believe essentially the same things I believe. From there I go home for dinner; then most nights I head over to church to dink around with one committee or another. My evenings are thus, if I'm not planted semiconscious in front of the TV, spent more often than not with people who pray the same prayers I pray, recite the same creeds I recite, listen to the same Christian music I listen to. All day and most every night, then, I'm surrounded by people who have a similar experience and understanding of God to mine, who are actively seeking to follow Jesus. And every once in a while, I want to smack one of them silly.

Sometimes I want to smack them because they're being so petty; sometimes, because I myself am feeling petty. Sometimes I want to smack them because they're behaving in a way that is self-destructive or harmful to the rest of us; sometimes, because I just feel like creating some turbulence. Sometimes they've taken a potshot at me, and I simply want to retaliate; sometimes I'm feeling burned by someone else, and they're an easier, safer outlet for my anger.

Limitless factors contribute to how our inner unsettledness manifests in our outward life, just as countless external catalysts force us to decide how other people will influence us—the scripts that over time have burrowed their way into our subconscious, the degrees of complexity our various relationships have taken on, the amount of responsibility or pressure we're carrying as an extension of the power or status or wealth we've acquired for ourselves. Jean Vanier recognizes the complexity of this internal process and the inevitability of its impact on how we relate to others. "There is an endless list of those we may exclude," he observes, and we might add those we may insult or demean or patronize or otherwise offend; "every one of us, we may be sure, is on someone's list."[3]

Brian Mahan suggests that our compassion—our capacity to care for other people—is inhibited by our ambitions, "setting limits on the reach and intensity of fellow-feeling." He recalls a thought experiment created by Walker Percy to illustrate this awkward psychosocial negotiation. The experiment is predicated on your run-in with your neighbor Charlie, who you've known to be very sick. "You look at him sympathetically" but then notice that he doesn't appear concerned or even unhealthy; he looks genuinely happy as he approaches you. "He has triple good news. His chest ailment turned out to be a hiatal hernia, not serious. He's got a promotion and is moving to Greenwich, where he can keep his boat in the water rather than on a trailer." So how do you feel? Percy gives you two options: (1) You feel unequivocally happy for your neighbor, or (2) you're happy for him but suddenly a little less happy for yourself. Those who picked the second option are given a continuum of seven choices to describe "which of the following news ... would make you feel better." The options range from your neighbor dropping dead on the spot to your saving your neighbor's life from a runaway garbage truck careening toward him. The spoiler answer is the seventh, in which you're generally happy, your neighbor is generally happy, and all of a sudden the city off in the distance is leveled by an earthquake, and only you and your neighbor have survived. Percy sums up the experiment: "In a word, how much good news about Charlie can you tolerate without compensatory catastrophes, rescues, and such?"[4]

An episode of the TV show *Friends* touched on this challenge of "fellow-feeling." Monica and Chandler are engaged to be married; their friends Rachel and Phoebe are talking over coffee about how happy they are for the couple. "I'm so happy—and not the least bit jealous," Rachel effuses. Before long she and Phoebe are figuring out the ratio of their joy compared to their jealousy, finally concluding that as long as joy makes up more than 50 percent of their feelings, they're okay.

Merton wondered in print whether, in the materially motivated, isolationist culture we've inherited, there is such a thing as "a genuine freedom for the person or only the irresponsibility of the atomized individual members of mass society?"[5] For Christians this matrix of our own developmental growth as persons and the social forces that still confront us are even more uncomfortable because we've left behind the scripts and values that organized them on our behalf; Jesus has led us out of the comfortable confines of Me-Ville and into the wide-open freedom of uncharted territory. Whatever turbulence we're feeling is part of the package, so we need to figure out ways of dealing with it.

STRANDED IN WE-VILLE

Our first impulse is to re-create the kind of institutional order we've left behind, to make the church that Jesus calls us into the rebound relationship that we expect to undo all the damage of the relationship we've just escaped. So rather than undertake the journey Jesus has us on, the journey that ultimately arrives us at his kingdom, we quickly relocate from Me-Ville to We-Ville. That's what Abraham's father did; Terah left "Ur of the Chaldees for the land of Canaan. But when they got as far as Haran, they settled down there.... He died in Haran" (Gen. 11:31–32). In the very next verse of the Bible, God told Abraham to get moving "for a land that I will show you" (Gen. 12:1), and eventually God showed him Canaan—the land that Terah was headed toward in the first place.

Lot, Abraham's nephew, had the same impulse. Immediately upon being rescued out of Sodom, a city doomed to destruction, Lot was ordered to head for the mountains. He replied, "Who knows what terrible thing might happen to me in the mountains.... That town is close enough to get to. It's a small town, hardly anything to it. Let me escape there" (Gen. 19:18–20).

The desire for security in the face of a sudden insecurity is overwhelming sometimes, causing us to disregard even the commands of

God or the rule of common sense in order to grasp on to something concrete, something immediate, some surrogate for what we suddenly lack.

The church, carrying as it does the title "body of Christ," very logically provides that surrogacy for a lot of people. Someone whose lifestyle has been totally at odds with what the Bible has to say about morality and ethics may become a Christian and say to herself, *I'm going to need all new friends. Everything I do with myself week in and week out needs to change.* Perhaps she's struggled with addictions, and her conversion involves a cold-turkey withdrawal from her drug of choice. She needs to clear the decks so she's not tempted back into her old way of life. Sounds sensible, right?

Not everybody has such a dramatic conversion, however, and some addictions and compulsions are more subtle than others. When I was in college, I threw myself into evangelical churchy kinds of things; I went to every chapel service at school and helped my friends to plan our own supplemental services. I drove a half hour every Sunday morning to a two-hour charismatic church service and actively recruited my friends throughout the week to join me. I stopped listening to secular music and started listening exclusively to Christian music—even though I thought most of it sucked. And after college I got involved in a high-school youth ministry to keep me busy and to keep those high-school kids from falling into the suburban sin patterns I'd so recently been rescued from.

Then my grandfather died. A deeply religious man with a large and boisterous family, his funeral would be a significant event. Priests all over the Midwest would attend his funeral out of respect for his son, their fellow priest. Family members three and four degrees removed from my grandfather's nucleus would be driving in from all over the country to give tribute to his memory. The first grandparent for most of his grandchildren to die, his funeral would be a seminal moment in the family history. But I had a gig.

At the time, I was playing saxophone for the high-school ministry's worship team. Handfuls of people were counting on me week in and week out to supplement the singing and guitar playing and drum beating and keyboard pounding with my own horn honking—and when horn honking wasn't appropriate, with more contemplative instruments like shaker eggs and the vibraslap.

The youth service was Sunday night; the funeral was Sunday morning. I was worried that I would not be able to do both. And I was sorely tempted to play the gig.

Eventually my brother convinced me that my place that weekend was with my family. But I think back to that moment every once in a while, because there were so many rationales available to me to justify staying to play the gig. Jesus, to begin with the most crass example, says point-blank: "Let the dead bury the dead." The notion was that a funeral is at best a look backward, a self-indulgent practice of weeping over what we've lost and remembering all the good times we've had. Meanwhile kids are still living and thus still in need of guidance that only a saxophone player can provide. Who could know for certain whether that one night, one honk from my horn might mark the turning point for some kid surrendering his life to God? How could I in good conscience walk away from that just to indulge my grief and enjoy my family?

Another more insidious rationale most likely fed the first and fueled the others: Jesus said that to love him we must hate our father and mother, the insinuation being that our families can sometimes get in the way of an authentic relationship with Christ. Many of the family members I would see at this funeral were at best distantly related; in fact I had no meaningful relationship at all with some of them. Maybe my family was my past; my church was, perhaps, my future.

More to the point, I think, however, was the fact that at the funeral I would be one of hundreds of mourners, but at the gig I would be the only saxophonist. Jean Vanier says that "we all have this drive to do things that will be seen by others as valuable, things that make us feel good about ourselves and give us a sense of being alive."[6] I could anticipate nothing at the funeral that would allow me to stand out, to make my mark; at the gig I would be on display, doing something I loved and was good at. At the funeral I would feel the curse of death; at the gig I would feel the sense of being alive. It's a wonder, really, that my brother was able to get through to me.

JESUS STANDS BETWEEN US

These are some of the dynamics that attend a relocation. We have to recalibrate, to continually get our bearings and reassure ourselves that we're not hopelessly lost. And so we grasp on to something concrete that can remind us again and again that it's going to be all right. That, I think, is why kids are so notoriously known for whining over and over again from the backseat, "Are we there yet?" We are no longer *here,* the place we know; and we're not quite *there,* the place we've been promised. How then shall we live? Who will deliver us from the car seat?

The writer of the letter to the Hebrews instructed his audience not to avoid "worshiping together as some do but spurring each other on, especially as we see the big Day approaching" (Heb. 10:25). But that need for reassurance can become an addiction to assurance, and the church that is meant to encourage can become an idol that corrupts.

Dietrich Bonhoeffer was well aware of this grasping after security and serenity that accompanies people's awakening to their faith. He calls their expectation of Christian life together a "wish dream":

> The serious Christian, set down for the first time in a Christian community, is likely to bring with him a very definite idea of what Christian life together should be and to try to realize it. But God's grace speedily shatters such dreams. Just as surely as God desires to lead us to a knowledge of genuine Christian fellowship, so surely must we be overwhelmed by a great disillusionment with others, with Christians in general, and, if we are fortunate, with ourselves.[7]

Imagine, for example, the excitement with which some Gentiles came to faith when they heard the apostle Paul preach. And imagine further, after hearing Paul talk about Jesus, then sharing a meal with Peter, who had walked on water at Jesus' command, who had been the first to recognize that Jesus was the Christ, the Son of God. And then imagine, when some Jewish believers were in town, bringing a meal to Peter only to be sent away because Jews do not associate with Gentiles. The disillusionment would be dramatic, I suspect, because not only had you been rejected by the leaders of the faith you've just left everything for, but you'd witnessed hypocrisy and duplicity being practiced by people who you thought were one degree removed from the Son of God. Paul called it like he saw it; Peter was "clearly out of line … that's how fearful he was" (Gal. 2:11–12).

Fortunately for the Galatians and for us, Christian community is, according to Bonhoeffer, "not an ideal which we must realize; it is rather a reality created by God in Christ in which we may participate."

The more clearly we learn to recognize that the ground and strength and promise of all our fellowship is in Jesus Christ alone, the more serenely shall we think of our fellowship and pray and hope for it.[8]

We're not ordered to create a community of God; rather we're invited into one. As such, we're not responsible to come up with a way of working together, although we are responsible to one another. As Merton puts it,

The power of friendship is great if it doesn't find all of its meaning in itself. If people expect too much from each other, they can do each other harm; and disappointment and bitterness can overpower love and even replace it.[9]

We learn how this new community operates, not by trial and error, but by observation and emulation; we allow Jesus to stand between us, interpreting our behaviors and identifying our motivations for each other.

Within the spiritual community there is never, nor in any way, any "immediate" relationship of one to another.... As only Christ can speak to me in such a way that I may be saved, so others, too, can be saved only by Christ himself. This means that I must release the other person from every attempt of mine to regulate, coerce, and dominate him with my love. The other person needs to retain his independence of me; to be loved for what he is, as one for whom Christ became man, died, and rose again.[10]

Jesus, remember, is *pro-me* and not just in relation to us but in relation to the countless others he's brought us into relationship with. As such, he gets us; he's hip to the human condition, so to speak. He was tempted in all things just as we were, but he didn't sin; instead, he became sin because he is *pro-me.*

That's something that we have in common with Christ: We are at our root each *pro-me.* This, remember, is perfectly natural; we know ourselves from our infancy to be distinct from all other things, and we are our own only constant companion—with the exception, of course, of our Lord and Savior. We come to trust him because he proves himself to be *pro-me;* we learn to appreciate the people he's put in our lives because we've begun to see them through his eyes.

BEWARE YOURSELF AND ONE ANOTHER

The same John who wrote in his gospel about how slow Peter was (both in a footrace and in the sense of having common sense) wrote of Jesus warning a skeptical audience, "How do you expect to get anywhere with God when you spend all your time jockeying for position with each other, ranking your rivals and ignoring God?" (John 5:44). His running competition with Peter notwithstanding, John recognized the danger of *invidious comparison,* the threat to our spiritual well-being that comes when we shove Jesus out of the center in order to get a better look at our friends, relatives, and, above all, rivals—to size them up, to ascertain what they have that we don't and what we have that they don't. To thus shove Jesus from his rightful place in relation to us is to dis*integrate* what God has brought together; the logical conclusion of this kind of dis*integration* is a more deeply entrenched sense of superbia than we earlier escaped:

I have what you have not. I am what you are not.…
Therefore you suffer and I am happy, you are despised and I
am praised, you die and I live; you are nothing and I am
something, and I am all the more something because you are
nothing. And thus I spend my life admiring the distance
between you and me.[11]

We're reduced to the condition of the not-quite-reformed demo-
niac Jesus warned us about:

When a corrupting spirit is expelled from someone, it
drifts along through the desert looking for an oasis, some
unsuspecting soul it can bedevil. When it doesn't find anyone, it says, "I'll go back to my old haunt." On return, it
finds the person swept and dusted, but vacant. It then runs
out and rounds up seven other spirits dirtier than itself and
they all move in, whooping it up. That person ends up far
worse than if he'd never gotten cleaned up in the first place.
(Luke 11:24–26)

Without Christ obstructing our view of others, we're inclined to
see them as threats, tools, or toys and ourselves as hero at war, master
craftsman at work, or innocent child at play. When I decided that I
was no longer a Catholic but had become an evangelical, I crafted a
story for myself: I was the hero of this story, of course, and my heroic
quest was the journey from Religion to Relationship. Those who made
my journey more complicated—the relatives who didn't understand
why I wouldn't go to mass anymore, the secularized friends who
thought I was being ridiculously pious, the professors who had seen

this sort of thing before and wanted to make sure I kept doing my homework—were to various degrees my nemeses, *antagonistas*. Those who made this transition easier for me—my evangelical friends, the church leaders who gladly accepted my help—were allies of course; but then again, my subconscious mused, it was one of Jesus' closest friends who ultimately betrayed him, so it's probably best to keep my guard up. I did so by making myself indispensible to the people in charge of the ministries I aligned myself with—they knew they could count on me because my faith, unlike the faith of Some People I Know, was not fickle. I shoved my way into the inner circle of the Coolest Christian in the Room so that by association I would be holier and hipper than thou.

The degree to which I had deluded myself in my journey of faith became most pronounced at my wedding, where my oldest friends and closest relatives sat in the aisles and my new, acceptably devout friends wore the tuxes and escorted the bridesmaids. Some of those new friends are still close friends, of course, but many of them are far removed from my life these days, at best, part of my Facebook network. Meanwhile my oldest friends and closest relatives are still part of my life—a plot twist in the narrative I'd constructed for myself but a perfectly natural reality if you think about it.

Such is our capacity to delude ourselves. Sara Groves reflected on our propensity to tell our stories in the most heroic way possible in her song "Know My Heart":

> Why do I pray— do I pray to say I prayed an hour?…
> Why do I help—do I want to hear my name called out?…
> Why do I serve—do I serve so others will serve me?

In these confessions she hits a point of clarity that creates a crisis: *Maybe I'm not as good as I think I am.* She's not alone at that crisis point. Taking a step back from our day-to-day decisions reveals the steady influence of superbia leaning into our lives. Consider giving blood, for example. I give blood four times a year, or roughly every thirteen weeks. It's simple: Every time I go in, I fill out a card that schedules me for my next visit. My phlebotomist (the person who takes my blood) is as routinized into my life as my dentist (the person who takes my teeth). But take a step back from this pattern I've established for myself, and ask why I do it.

I could say that I do it because it's easy to keep doing and inconvenient to stop doing, because I would then open myself to shame-inducing telemarketing calls persistently recruiting me back into blood donation.

I could say that I do it because I enjoy talking with my phlebotomist and hearing the latest about her husband's band, a tribute to the Ramones, Gabba Gabba Hey[12]

I could say that I do it because every time I go I'm guaranteed one of those beef-and-cheese snack packs and a nutty brownie, treats I would never purchase for myself but are generously doled out at the blood donation office, and that for every four donations I'm rewarded with some very useful gift: a thermos, a sweatshirt, a blanket, a coffee mug— all things that warm me up and make me happy.

I could say that giving blood is the right thing to do, that by giving blood I emulate Christ, who gave his blood to save us all.[13]

I could say any and all of these things because they are all, to one degree or another, true reasons for why I regularly donate blood. But when asked, I'm most tempted to offer the most pious response— even when I'm wearing my Heartland Blood Services Windbreaker and wiping cheese and brownie residue from my lips.

That's four times a year, but these ethical instincts occur on a daily basis as well. Where I work, I tend to park in the spot farthest from the entrance. I've done that since I started working there. I do so for a number of reasons: Some people are in poorer health than I am and would thus benefit from parking closer to the door; I need every bit of exercise I can get, and a slightly longer walk from my car to my desk can only help; I want the status of my own parking place, and the parking space that people would least likely fight me for is the one farthest from the office; by parking as far from the door as possible, I follow the guidance of Jesus, who counseled his followers to take the seat at a gathering with the lowest status so that they can be invited to a higher status, rather than taking a seat with a high status and then being displaced when someone more important arrives; and finally, I want the status of being the guy who puts everybody else first, who voluntarily takes the last place. Over time I've identified all these impulses running through my mind as I pull into our parking lot. It's amazing I ever get out of my car.

I'm not alone either. The prophet Isaiah, the apostle Paul, the reformer Martin Luther, and countless other followers of Jesus down through the ages have hit that crisis point, questioning our ethical impulses, only to be reassured yet again that we are loved by God regardless of our patterns and quirks, that in Jesus Christ, God is *pro-me*—and in the words of Paul, "If God is for us, who can be against us?" (Rom. 8:31 NIV).

Certainly not people who are looking at us through the filter of Jesus, which is part of the reason Jesus takes his place at the center. It's not the only reason, of course—he stands at the center because that's his rightful place—but when Jesus is in his rightful place, the rest of us gradually fall into place ourselves.

Confession is our way of restoring Jesus to the center. That's why we are better off confessing not only in private but also in the company of our fellow sinners who have come to love us: Confession is a recognition of the truth set in the context of a loving relationship. Scripture tells us that the steadfast love of the Lord never changes; our instinct tells us (even when our experience might tell us otherwise) that those who love us, even when they've been offended by us, stick with us. Those who love us—and I include God in this circle—know from direct experience that we are sinners, that we regularly fall short of being the kind of people we or they would like us to be. They've felt the sting of our betrayal, suffered the wounds of our occasional indifference, chuckled compassionately at the absurdity of our folly. And they're still there, all along.

Of course, they're simultaneously living out their own story, and in their self-narration we've filled some role for them that is only at best partly true: Perhaps there are times, even long periods, where they see us as a threat or a tool or even a toy. For some reason we're likewise able to ride out those passing moments, because we have committed ourselves to loving them. And this we know, from the pen of the apostle John, who was so easily agitated by the apostle Peter: Love comes from God.

In confession we acknowledge that our view of ourselves is, like the view others have of us, incomplete, clouded by our cluttered narratives. In the abstract Thomas Merton was perfect—a serene monk living in solitude and writing some of the most profound insights into the human soul of the twentieth century. But those who loved him knew him to be easily irritated, prone to delusions of self-importance, argumentative. And they loved him anyway because they saw him as Christ saw him.

Similarly, in the abstract Henri Nouwen was perfect—a quiet soul, doing the kinds of things that all of us know intuitively to be the right thing. But those who loved him knew him to be frustratingly needy, clingy, and insecure. In his *Genesee Diary* he confesses, "The irony was that I always wanted to be alone to work, but when I was finally left alone, I couldn't work and started to become more morose, angry, sour, hateful, bitter and complaining."[14] Those closest to him—and I include God in this—recognized these tendencies in Nouwen and loved him anyway, because they saw him through the filter of Christ, who stood at the center.

Even so profound a saint as Mother Teresa—perfect in the abstract—was known by those who loved her to struggle throughout life with the paradox that a loving God stood watch over a hateful world. And they prayed for her and supported her and encouraged her because they loved her as Christ did, from the center.

Jean Vanier looks at the witness of people like Teresa, Nouwen, and Merton, and you and me, and the entire family of God, and defines community primarily as communion, which Jesus made sacred by his sacrifice.

> Communion is not a fixed state, it is an ever-growing
> and deepening reality that can turn sour if one person tries to
> possess the other…. Communion is mutual vulnerability and
> openness one to the other. It is liberation for both, indeed,
> where both are allowed to be themselves.[15]

WE NEED EACH OTHER

I have a rock in my house. I got it at a small-group meeting. It's big—it's clearly not there by accident. Written on the rock is the phrase "We need each other." I believe that—we need each other because it's so frustratingly easy to reduce each other from three dimensions to two, to look at one another as nothing more than toys, tools, or threats in whatever narrative we're constructing for ourselves in the moment. We need each other because it's so frustratingly easy to shove Jesus out of the center and to face the world and all its inhabitants alone. We need each other because we need love, and love is the heart of communion.

But we also need to not need each other. Just as we're able to dehumanize each other in even so pious a distraction as our personal journey toward God's kingdom, we're shockingly capable of de-divinizing God in our idolatry of human relationships. Bonhoeffer famously warned, "Let him who cannot be alone beware of community," because community, in the self-narrative of such a person, shoves Jesus out of the center and recalibrates the person's whole universe. We veer off our journey toward God's kingdom and settle for another of its suburbs, We-Ville. Spend enough time there, and we are exposed to the unfiltered fallenness of even the most devout followers of Jesus. And we discover that We-Ville is, sadly, only a dressed-up version of Me-Ville. We're back where we started, and more disillusioned for it.

Bonhoeffer goes on, however:

> But the reverse is also true: *Let him who is not in community beware of being alone.* Into the community you were called…. You are not alone, even in death, and on the Last Day you will be only one member of the great congregation of Jesus Christ. If you scorn the fellowship of the brethren, you reject the call of Jesus Christ, and thus your solitude can only be hurtful.[16]

Wherever God is taking us, he's taking us together. It's tempting to look at such a great crowd and say, "Let's build a city and settle down so we can enjoy one another. Let's stop moving and start living!" But God knows, and in our best moments we know, our journey is not yet complete until we all arrive together in a city not made by human hands—the land we've been promised: the city of God.

(• ESCAPE ROUTES •)

CONFESSION

When we confess our sins before a brother-Christian, we are mortifying the
pride of the flesh.

—Dietrich Bonhoeffer, *The Cost of Discipleship*

If you want to really experience Christian community, get into the
habit of confession. Make yourself vulnerable to someone else, and see what
happens. Brian Mahan writes:

> We do not transcend our ambitions so much by claiming to
> have already risen above them as by slowly, patiently, and faithfully
> working our way through them, at ground level and in the company
> of our friends.[17]

Consider your existing relationships, and think of who is most likely to
hang with you even when you're being unlikable, even when you're disclosing
the darkest parts of yourself. What would it take to consecrate that relationship so that you can help one another interpret your stories, expose your
self-delusions, recalibrate your universe so that Christ is still in the center?
My relationships that serve that function have taken years to cultivate, but
they each began with a sacred moment in which one or the other or both of us
said: "We need each other."

Don't do this haphazardly. Once you've realized that you need someone,
look for ways to consecrate the relationship. Read and analyze prayers of

confession from the Book of Common Prayer or other sources, and discuss
with your sacred friends what is most important to these prayers, what res-
onates most in them with your need for a right orientation toward God and
the world. Create time and space to come together and speak freely and
soberly about how you're seeing the world lately. Commit yourselves to listening to one another while you sort through what's still tethering you to
Me-Ville and what's tempting you off the road to God's city.

Don't be salacious; details of how many lustful thoughts you've had or a
meticulous inventory of how many naughty words you've said in the past week
miss the point: We don't need to become good nearly as much as we need to
live in light of our finiteness, our inability to make ourselves right with God.[18]
By focusing on the gory details of our failings, we not only set a heretical
agenda of "becoming sinless" but also indulge a morbid self-fascination, disregard the virtue of modesty, and tempt our confession partners toward the
invidious comparison that sends them back toward Me-Ville. Bonhoeffer wrote:

> "Truthfulness" does not mean uncovering everything that
> exists. God himself made clothes for men.... Exposure is cynical,
> and although the cynic prides himself on his exceptional honesty, or
> claims to want truth at all costs, he misses the crucial fact that since
> the fall there *must* be reticence and secrecy.... What is secret may
> be revealed *only* in confession.[19]

Remember that Jesus consecrated his followers and, by extension, all
of us to be priests for one another—to bind those sins that are clearly
binding, to loose those sins that have a choke hold on those we love.
Above all we're to support one another—to have one another's back and to
help carry one another's burdens. We are all together a kingdom of priests,
and it's our responsibility to serve that priestly office for one another.

Ask one another questions such as the following:

- What do you think God is directing you toward these days? Is that exciting for you? Scary? Uninteresting?
- What other directions are you getting these days? In what ways do they
  overlap with what you think God is telling you? In what ways do they
  conflict?
- What is tempting you from the path God has called you on toward a path
  of less resistance?
- What would help you to stay on the right path?
- What would you like me to do for you?

GETTING IN THE WAY OF JESUS

And really, that's pretty much it. Jesus comes to us in our kingdom of self and calls us out. Then he collects us together as he leads us to the city of God. Pretty simple, really.

We like to overthink matters. Overthinking is akin to overachieving—the kind of sin you confess when you're asked at a job interview about your greatest weakness. Thinking is given props in the Bible—"To search out a matter is the glory of kings"—but also put in its proper context: "It is the glory of God to conceal a matter" (Prov. 25:2 NIV). It's even a staple of Christian thought, from the Bible to Augustine to Calvin to Tozer to today, that we come to know ourselves better as we come to know God, and we come to know God better as we come to know ourselves. So Christianity affirms curiosity and the quest for knowledge. But another staple of Christian thought is that God is wrapped in unapproachable light, that his ways are higher than our ways, that we can never figure out or outfigure God. When we venture into such arrogant thinking, our curiosity and quest for knowledge are getting the better of us.

I saw a sketch once where people arrived in heaven and had the opportunity for some Q & A with Saint Peter. These new residents in God's city were powerfully curious and asked all the most niggling questions that keep us awake at night, questions like "Why do good people suffer?" "Why does God allow evil?" "Why do I have an appendix?" Saint Peter very happily and concisely answered each question, but the audience couldn't hear his response: A loud horn or some other sound effect would drown out whatever he was saying. The interruption would end in time for the audience to hear Peter's guests say something like, "That makes perfect sense! Why didn't I think of that?" The message of the sketch was that God has an answer for every question. In the meantime we're knowledgeable enough, by God's grace, to get by; curious enough, by God's grace, to keep moving.

We're also knowledgeable enough and curious enough to be dangerous—to ourselves and others. God calls us to obedience because he's God, which means he's boss, but also because we are so vulnerable to such disobedience. It was human self-importance manifested in curiosity that Satan exploited when tempting Adam and Eve to disobey God and eat from the forbidden tree. It was human curiosity alongside puffed-up knowledgeability that led a Levite to reach out a hand to steady an ark that he knew was not to be touched. It's human curiosity alongside a cocky self-assurance that compels us to click on that dubious link or drink that second drink. Left to ourselves we couldn't survive our own curiosity, our own thirst for knowledge. God conceals enough, by his grace, to keep it interesting.

Meanwhile the ultimate mystery has already been explained: The farther from Me-Ville and closer to Thee-Ville that we get, the more we notice the evidence that we're actually already there, that God has existed all along, that the earth is the Lord's and the fullness thereof.

The basic reality of God is plain enough. Open your eyes and there it is! By taking a long and thoughtful look at what

God has created, people have always been able to see what their eyes as such can't see: eternal power, for instance, and the mystery of his divine being. (Rom. 1:19–20)

The sprawl and the smog of Me-Ville effectively shroud God's sovereignty over his creation, and so we don't start to pick up on it until we get outside the city limits. And the full disclosure of God's reign is still off in the horizon. Between here and there—between now, when we live aware of God's kingdom and learn to reconcile ourselves to it, and that day when we will find that we've been here all along, encircled by God's grace, transformed by his goodness—by faith we walk and walk and walk.[1]

Long walks are a significant part of a Christian heritage. Jesus' ministry was largely a walking ministry—from Bethlehem to Egypt to Nazareth to Cana to Capernaum to Jerusalem and to Gethsemane and ultimately, when his followers took the baton, to the ends of the earth. Prior to that, exiled Israelites walked from a desolated Jerusalem to points east and south and north, only to later walk back and restore the city. Prior to that, the patriarchs walked from Ur to Haran and from Haran to Canaan and from Canaan to Egypt. And in perhaps the most significant walk of the Christian faith, the Israelites walked out of Egypt and into the Promised Land.

Led by Moses, the Israelites walked by the millions across rivers, up and down mountains, and over deserts for forty years—and as Moses reminded them late in their journey, their sandals never wore out. They carried with them the bones of Joseph, the patriarch who had delivered them safely into Egypt in the first place but who knew their ultimate destination lay elsewhere. Joshua was with them, the upstart leader who would one day take Moses' place and oversee the next leg of their journey. Before them was God, directing their path by day and by night. In the midst of them was God, reassuring them with his presence in the tabernacle and by his presence, laying down ground rules for how to live responsibly as a free people in God's kingdom. Behind them was God, routing the Egyptians who chased after them and prodding the Israelites forward. They kept well nourished from year one to year forty; they made alliances and defeated enemies; they made mistakes and suffered the consequences. They walked their way through all of this by faith.

Walking by faith takes practice. We learn by the accident of our own overexertion and by the example of other people's ambition what wears us out too quickly, and so we learn to pace ourselves. We learn by the accident of our own disobedience and by the example of other people's falls from grace how easy it is to drift off course, and so we learn to follow directions. We learn by accident and by example that although everyone else is not necessarily right, we're occasionally wrong, and so we learn to rely not on ourselves or other tourists but on the tour guide out in front.

Walking by faith, we learn about ourselves, we learn about the human condition, and we learn about God. The key to this gradual transformation is to keep a sober judgment of ourselves—our proneness to wander back toward Me-Ville and our tendency to act rashly out of our desire to be thought well of—but more importantly to keep Jesus in view. The key to doing both is to regularly get in his way.

TAKING VOWS WITHOUT TAKING THEM TOO SERIOUSLY

We've undeniably not saved ourselves from superbia; only God, we've discovered on our way out and on our regular sorties back in, is capable of finally and completely delivering us. Bonhoeffer writes,

To deny oneself is to be aware only of Christ and no
more of self, to see only him who goes before and no more
the road which is too hard for us.... All that self-denial can
say is: "He leads the way, keep close to him."[2]

As such, self-denial isn't a willful act so much as it is a consequence
of Christ having taken his rightful place in our frame of reference. Self-
denial is essentially resignation, an acknowledgment that we ultimately
can't know what we're doing or where we're going. "He," not we, "leads
the way." The best thing we can do is to "keep close to him."

We find it easy, however, to see this act of resignation as some noble
act of covenantal devotion. We lay our crowns at the feet of Jesus in
some opulent ceremony worthy of kings and queens such as we. So we
turn those moments of resignation into vows of faithfulness, like Peter's
promise that he'll die for Jesus, when in truth he was hours away from
forsaking the Son of God.

Some Christian teens wear a wedding band as a symbol that they
will wait to marry before they have sex. Premarital sex is dangerous and
often traumatizing, and efforts to contain the hypersexualization of
youth culture are praiseworthy. But the fact remains that most kids who
make these covenant promises fail to keep them. They're left with a ring
that regularly reminds them that God in his wisdom didn't keep them
and their partner off one another.

They're not alone; people make financial commitments to churches
(and by extension, to God) and fail to keep them. The divorce rate is
evidence that the marriage covenant, pledged before God and family
and friends and the state, is hard to keep.

Nevertheless, we continue to make vows because the notion of making promises to one another, and all the more so to God, strikes us as

noble and right. It's not as though, for example, we're promising to be a screwup; we're determining what are true and noble things that we could commit ourselves to, and then we're committing ourselves to those things. Failing to keep such commitments can be discouraging, but it can also serve as a reminder that we're finite, fallen, unable to save ourselves. We need a deliverer. The Bible testifies to the fact that no one consistently keeps such commitments; Jesus suggested that the people who seemed to manage to keep their commitments—the Pharisees and the other religious elite of his day—were lying to the rest of us as well as to themselves. That, the Bible tells us, is one of the things that separates us from God: God keeps his commitments, and God abides in the truth.

SINNING BOLDLY AND FAILING WELL

Martin Luther is said to have told his friend Philip Melanchthon, who was tirelessly meticulous in his attempt to avoid doing anything wrong, "For God's sake, sin a little. God deserves to forgive you for something!" It's a good line, but it draws attention to the greater danger that lies behind our attempts to deliver ourselves from evil: "The greatest of tyrannies are all ... based on the postulate that *there should never be any sin.*"[3]

Of course there will be sin, is the contention of the Bible. The initial fall of the human race inaugurated the world of sin, and in such a world things will not be the way they're supposed to be. Dallas Willard recognizes that our failure to accept the terms of life in a sinful world actually cheapens the gospel and stalls us in our movement toward the kingdom God intends.

> History has brought us to the point where the Christian message is thought to be *essentially* concerned *only* with how

to deal with sin: with wrongdoing or wrong-being and its
effects. Life, our actual existence, is not included in what is
now presented as the heart of the Christian message, or it is
included only marginally. That is where we find ourselves
today....

When we examine the broad spectrum of Christian
proclamation and practice, we see that the only thing made
essential on the right wing of theology is forgiveness of the
individual's sins. On the left it is removal of social or struc-
tural evils. The current gospel then becomes a "gospel of sin
management." Transformation of life and character is *no* part
of the redemptive message. Moment-to-moment human reality in its depths is not the arena of faith and eternal living.[4]

To think of our faith beyond the constraints of sin management is
to think of where God is leading us and where God has thus far led us
from. Moses called out to the Israelites from Mount Sinai to tell them
that they were no longer slaves; the gospel of sin management reads
his speech in Exodus and sees a list of rules we're called to obey, but the
broader picture is the change of self-understanding God was calling
the Israelites to: They were now a free people, under the sovereignty of
an unequaled God. They needed to stop subsisting like slaves—driven
by immediate circumstances, indulging themselves in little vices and
petty disputes, hoarding whatever power and privilege they could
scrape together, looking out for number one under the assumption that
nobody else was going to and start enjoying the privileges and
embracing the responsibilities of life in the kingdom of God. They
would keep walking because God was calling them to walk, but they
should walk with confidence and resolve, knowing that they're being

led to a good and pleasant place where they'll dwell all together in peace and security.

Paul made a similar speech to the Corinthian church:

> Take a good look, friends, at who you were when you got called into this life. I don't see many of "the brightest and the best" among you, not many influential, not many from high-society families. Isn't it obvious that God deliberately chose … "nobodies" to expose the hollow pretensions of the "some-bodies"? That makes it quite clear that none of you can get by with blowing your own horn before God. Everything that we have—right thinking and right living, a clean slate and a fresh start—comes from God by way of Jesus Christ. That's why we have the saying, "If you're going to blow a horn, blow a trumpet for God." (1 Cor. 1:26–31)

Toot toot. Getting in the way of Jesus reminds us of our finiteness but immediately thereafter reminds us that we've now been called beyond that, that out of love for us God is leading us to a new and better place. The best we can do for ourselves and those around us and, really, the whole world is to say, "He leads the way. Follow him."

"JESUS OR NOT JESUS?"

The most common means of getting in the way of Jesus is, of course, by accident. This happens all the time—mostly because people are so self-involved that they trip on Jesus and assume he is "Not Jesus." The trick is to be aware of it and ready for it.

Peter's postcrucifixion strategy was to recover a normal life, to busy himself with profitable distractions. Going fishing would keep his mind occupied and would put food on his table. Going fishing was the closest thing to status quo that Peter knew, and so once his adventure with Jesus was over, Peter settled back into the status quo and went fishing.

Jesus showed up on the beach while Peter and a few other disciples were out on the lake. They'd already run into each other since Jesus' resurrection, and Jesus had offered compelling evidence that it was him, not a ghost, alive. Resurrection from the dead is pretty far removed from the status quo. So once Jesus made his presence known, Peter had a few options available to him:

1. He could assume that, despite all evidence to the contrary, what he knew of human physiology was correct, that someone who has died cannot still be considered alive, and he could disregard the strange man he had seen in the upper room and has now seen on the beach as "Not Jesus." By doing so he could finally reestablish his normal life, putting the "King of Israel" behind him and looking out once again for number one.

2. He could indulge his skepticism and go in for a closer look, thus strengthening his reputation as courageous leader while avoiding the label of gullible dope.

3. He could let someone else take the lead, row himself and his colleagues back to shore, and keep his dignity intact.

4. He could jump in a lake.

Peter chose option 4, swimming to Jesus while the other disciples dutifully rowed the boat ashore. By doing so, he risked the dramatic disappointment he would experience if Jesus was actually Not Jesus; he also risked the embarrassment of having his unbridled enthusiasm put on display by his more reserved friends. He even risked rejection from Jesus, whom he'd betrayed three times, once he reached the beach.[5]

Peter's risk here was mitigated by the potential gain. He was about to be reunited with the man he had given three years of his life to. He was about to have breakfast with a man who had once been dead. He was about to meet the Son of God again. He just had to get himself back out of Me-Ville.

Me-Ville is a place we will visit again and again and again over the course of our lives. It's such an interesting place for such curious people as us, such a safe place for such insecure people as us. In Me-Ville we can safely and comfortably look out for number one, which every once in a while will sound like the most sensible thing in the world to do.

But the farther Jesus leads us from Me-Ville to the place he has prepared for us, the less sensible it is to go back, and the less fulfilling each visit will be. By the time Jesus caught Peter fishing here, Peter had seen too much to settle for his former life. He'd seen Jesus do miracles Peter couldn't do and say things Peter never would have thought of. When you notice Jesus, especially where you weren't expecting to see him, you notice that what he's doing and saying are a lot more interesting, a lot more creative than what you're doing and saying.

So notice Jesus. Karen Mains identifies four ways that God makes himself noticeable in our lives: (1) obvious answers to prayer, (2) unexpected evidence of care, (3) unexpected help to do the right thing, and (4) moments of serendipity. She treats the exercise of identifying these divine interventions as a game: the God Hunt.

Finding God incognito in the world is not a ho-hum
proposition. It is delight. It is joy. It is wonder. It is a childlike

wiggling anticipation that somewhere, any moment, just
around the next corner, when you least expect it, the Divine is
going to jump out.[6]

Sometimes it's not exciting, of course, because of the day or the
week or the year you're having. After I finished school, I moved to a
town where I knew my girlfriend and no one else. I had no job prospects
and no place to live for at least a couple of months. My first year out of
college I struggled to get my career started, and I developed a keen sense
of shame as a consequence. After a while I prayed to God, telling him
I didn't believe in him anymore. I was headed back to Me-Ville, thank
you very much.

The next day I drove around and heard song after song on the radio
telling me that all would be well. I wasn't in the mood for "all will be
well," of course, seeing as I had just denied the existence of God to his
face, but the songs were there nonetheless. And a couple of conversations with friends who had no idea how I felt reassured me nevertheless
that all would be well. All wasn't well anytime soon after that day, but
by the end of the day I had the vague notion that eventually it would
be and, beyond that, that God did, in fact, exist.

John Ortberg, borrowing from John Calvin, would see my experience as an example of how God draws us in on the process toward
spiritual maturity, which amounts to trusting that God is there and
knowing God when we see him.

> God is gracious to communicate to us even at the point
> of our immaturity in a way that we can understand. John
> Calvin has a beautiful metaphor for this: ... [as a nurse con-
> soles a crying child,] God stoops. God lisps.

Our job is to be ruthless about saying yes when we
believe God is speaking to us. Every time we do, we will get a
little more sensitive to hearing him the next time. Our mind
becomes a little more receptive, a little more tuned in to
God's channel.[7]

Once we've started to notice God, even if our first encounter was
entirely by accident, we can make a game of it, like Karen Mains, to
keep one eye out for where God is living and active in our day-to-day
life and to say, "Gotcha!" when we notice him—to acknowledge that
even in a self-centered world, Christ has not stepped out of his rightful
place in the center of it.

Maturity comes gradually as our "Gotchas" give way to the question
"Now what?" We eventually wonder why God is there or, more precisely, why God is making himself noticeable to us. "Now what?" leads
us into the kind of conduct that he has ordained for us. Oddly enough,
we don't even need to be conscious of it; as far as we know, we're just
playing a game, having fun.

Peter had matured some by the time Jesus came to him in a dream
and asked him to eat food that good Jewish boys don't eat. Peter had a
few options available to him in that moment:

1. He could have told himself, "You're dreaming," and disre-
   garded the whole thing.
2. He could have decided Jesus had finally asked too much of
   him and instructed him to get out of his head.
3. He could have told Jesus, "Yes, Master," and started eating.
4. He could have had a nice, long conversation with Jesus.

Peter isn't brilliant by any measure, but when Jesus showed up unawares, Peter noticed. He also noticed the presenting problem, which involved not only Jewish dietary laws but also the whole posture of Jewish Christians toward non-Jewish Christians. So he didn't simply obey Jesus; he worked out what Jesus was telling him. And later, when Peter was awake, he noticed God at work again among non-Jewish Christians and led the early church through one of its most complex, delicate controversies.

He did so relatively unconsciously; his left hand, you might say, didn't know what his right hand was doing. His report to the Jerusalem church of his experience is not at all self-serving; he represents himself not as the guru who has guided himself into a new enlightenment but simply as a guy who has woken up from an interesting dream. He somehow did what we need to somehow be doing: noticing Jesus during downtimes and during busy times and figuring out the why behind the encounter.

QUIET TIME

Much has been made of the quiet time—a repeated, protected period of time each day to be with God. The quiet time is sacred practice for many, a barometer of how their day will go and a baseline for how their faith stacks up against the faith of others. During a given quiet time a person might read a passage from Scripture or spend some time in prayer or sing songs of worship or read some devotional thoughts by a favorite author or, really, any number of other things. Many people set aside a part of their morning for their quiet time, while others reserve it for the evening—the evening, perhaps, because it's an opportunity to reflect on the events of the day, the morning because it gives God the firstfruits of the day.

That's quiet time as a liturgy; to the extent that we've established and sanctified a regular practice such as this one, we've set up a devout rhythm to our lives. But any liturgy carries with it the temptation toward conceit. I used to ask people, "How's your quiet time going?" because that's what people in my church talked about when they wanted to know how someone was doing spiritually. But before long I realized that I didn't really know how to answer that question myself, and how I answered that question was really, really important to my reputation in the church. Answering with not enough activities or the wrong resources or simply an insufficient enthusiasm would affect my ranking on the church's unofficial spiritual leader board. I once met a guy who told me that he was eventually nudged out of a church because he told a friend that he had started reading a certain author as part of his devotional practice.[8]

Meanwhile the day has plenty more "quiet time" where that came from, and somehow those other quiet moments have escaped sanctification, have gone unliturgized because they are somehow unremarkable. But it's those unremarkable moments that can be particularly pregnant with the presence of God—more so often than a designated "quiet time" that we meticulously mark as much for our friends and spiritual authorities as we do for ourselves. Brother Lawrence, for example, has become famous over the centuries for his willingness to look for God in the mundane, to revel in the anonymous, undocumented encounters with God as they occurred during everyday tasks. David Hansen, in his book *Long Wandering Prayer,* makes the audacious claim that we can be in continual conversation with God simply by keeping our eyes and ears and spirit open as we make our way through the day—even through the golf course.

The Bible affirms this notion that there are quiet encounters with

God that extend far beyond the ritualized quiet times that we allot for ourselves:

- Moses received the call to deliver Egypt not from a prophet while he worshipped in a temple, but from a burning bush while he was alone, tending his flocks.[9]
- Samuel heard from God not during a ritual service but in the middle of the night while he was trying to sleep.
- Elijah heard from God not in the temple of the Lord but on the run from the queen.
- Paul had a run-in with Jesus along the highway long before he preached about God from the Aeropagus.

This is not to say, of course, that God chooses not to speak through the rituals that his people have established for themselves. God is, however, not bound by those rituals; as Carl Jung put it, "Bidden or unbidden, God is present."[10] A. W. Tozer suggests that this understanding of God's presence is only reasonable: "That God is here both Scripture and reason declare. It remains only for us to learn to realize this in conscious experience."[11]

So one means of getting in the way of Jesus is by looking for the intrusion of God into quiet times—both sacred and casual. Some people do it with a simple prayer—"Jesus, Son of David, have mercy on me, a sinner,"—said intermittently throughout the day. Some people do it by praying a liturgy of the hours—four or five formal prayers at designated times of day; by increasing the number of liturgized moments in a day, the logic goes, the more casual moments are more regularly anchored in devotion. Others place visual cues to remind them that they are accompanied through their day by God—a Scripture verse on their computer desktop, a cross on their wall or around their neck. Whatever helps you to relocate your thoughts. Frederick Buechner recognized the value of such disciplined movement through our ordinary days:

> There is no event so commonplace but that God is present within it, always hiddenly, always leaving you room to recognize him or not to recognize him, but all the more fascinatingly because of that, all the more compellingly and hauntingly…. In the boredom and pain of it no less than in the excitement and gladness: touch, taste, smell your way to the holy and hidden heart of it because in the last analysis all moments are key moments, and life itself is grace.[12]

LOUD TIME

That's quiet time. Sometimes, however, you just have to get loud. Another side effect of the cult of the quiet time, besides the conformity pressure and compartmentalizing of our life with Jesus already discussed, is the neglect of the devotional value of time spent throughout the day in the company of others. I named my blog "Loud Time" for just this reason: because God is not some imaginary friend who goes into hiding whenever our flesh-and-blood friends and neighbors show up. Jesus, as a matter of fact, sanctifies every gathering with his presence: "Wherever two or more of you are gathered in my name, there I am in the midst of them."

By privileging solitude—"quiet time"—over fellowship as a means of identifying God at work, we privilege our own instincts over the instincts of others. As a consequence we leave ourselves vulnerable to blind spots of our own tendencies toward superbia, so that our moral and ethical judgments are rooted not so much in devotion to God but in sanctified self-interest. Bonhoeffer is so bold as to suggest that "truth happens *only* in community."[13] Theologian Vince Bacote puts it slightly more cynically: "History has shown that people aren't trustworthy when thinking about themselves."[14] Thomas Merton—a cloistered monk, mind you—cautioned his readers to "not flee to solitude from the community. Find God first in the community, then He will lead you to solitude."[15] It was this prior understanding of his faith as communal first, solitary second, that framed Merton's outlook in compassion rather than derision:

> I have learned ... to look back into the world with
> greater compassion, seeing those in it not as alien to myself,
> not as peculiar and deluded strangers, but as identified with
> myself.[16]

When we neglect the devotional potential of loud time, we lose sight not only of our bonded relationship to one another, we also lose sight of God's communal, kingdom-building agenda—and his tendency to look for occasions to celebrate. Jesus preaches often about the banquet at the end of time, in which the wicked and the foolish are not those who party too hard but those who think they're too important for such frivolities. Some of God's most momentous interventions in history are marked by celebration:

- The Israelites sang songs of praise on the far side of the Red
  Sea once God had delivered them finally from the Egypt-
  ian army.

- David danced like a crazy man at the head of a parade as
  the ark of the covenant was brought to its resting place in
  Jerusalem.
- The Israelites celebrated with remarkable vigor at the dedication of the first temple.
- At the dedication of the second temple, they celebrated just
  as vigorously, with cheers interspersing with tears to mark
  the occasion for miles around.
- Jesus entered Jerusalem to the shouts of an adoring crowd,
  and he suggested that even the rocks would make some
  noise if they could.
- The Holy Spirit descended on the early church on Pentecost
  and created such a cacophony of celebration that thousands
  of people converted to a faith that had barely taken shape.

Loud times may offend the sensibilities of the private, reserved, self-conscious citizens of Me-Ville, but they're the hallmark of a God who is actively reconciling the world to himself.

Like quiet times, loud times happen throughout our days and our weeks, but we have certain sanctified experiences of such life together: the worship service, the small-group Bible study, the prayer breakfast. That's all well and good, but what would it be like to sanctify a spontaneous moment together—to be like Peter, who didn't know what hit him and his friends on Pentecost Sunday but hopped to his feet and declared that God was with them, bringing thousands to faith in Christ? We might pray in advance of our casual time together—going out with a group, having friends over for dinner, going into meetings at work, or any number of other casual encounters—that we'd see one another through Jesus, that we'd keep an eye out for how Jesus might be working in and among us as a group.

That's a risky business, of course: Jesus might be gearing up to confront one of us or all of us about bad decisions we're making or to direct us into more uncomfortable intentional encounters—with the poor, for example, or the elderly, or the sick—alone or together. But if we're committed to the notion that God doesn't save only each of us but all of us and that God is pulling us into a community together, and if we're further committed to the notion that God acts out of love for us and works through us to communicate that love to one another—then even the most difficult encounter, the most nerve-racking news is framed in grace. When we enter into our relationships assured that God is *pro-me* and consequently pro-us, we can more confidently remember that not even we, ultimately, can be against us.

WHAT'S IN A DAY

When we look for opportunities to get in the way of Jesus, our quiet times and our loud times work together to define the day for us. When we've been conscious of God's presence with us, we find that both our times of being quiet and our times of being loud have served as a witness to the goodness of God. They make an impact on the culture as a result: Citizens of Me-Ville notice the odd silence that follows us around—this isn't mere silent self-absorption; it's sanctified, edge-of-your-seat stuff, anticipation that something's stirring, attentiveness to the movement of God's Spirit. Citizens of Me-Ville likewise notice loud time when it comes: How could they not, really, when people who have gone about their day with such intentional quiet energy come together and bring the noise with them?

Forty years after leaving Egypt, the Israelites finally entered the Promised Land, where they came upon the walled city of Jericho. This would be a setback to any observer, but the Israelites, following God's lead and the instruction of Joshua, walked around the city in silence over and over and over, making no move to attack or retreat. Imagine being on the wall of Jericho, watching this steady, silent procession: How could you not watch, really? And then the order came from Joshua: "Shout! For the Lord your God has given you the city!" And the Israelites shouted, and the walls came down, and the people of God took possession of the land God had promised them.

Again, imagine being an observer to this process. This isn't the result of superior military strategy on the part of the Israelites; it's not even the fundamental flaws in Jericho's design that are at fault. This is miraculous—a divine intervention that passes judgment even while offering a new promise. God has proved himself more powerful than any mere city. The gates even of hell couldn't stand against this God, much less the meager walls of Me-Ville. The future lies elsewhere, wherever he deems to take us; and however rough the road that stretches out before us we know by faith that it will be marked with moments of quiet intimacy with God and moments of loud celebration with the people of God.

MARKING TIME

One of the occupational hazards of a long walk is the temptation to switch on autopilot, to conserve energy by not paying attention to where we are in the moment or where we might be headed. This can happen at the individual level and at the level of community; I might start drifting back toward Me-Ville; you and everybody else might see it happening but decide that reeling me back in is someone else's job. The net effect is that a gathered group of people begins to dissipate, and people on a trek toward God's city are left merely wandering in the desert.

The challenge is to build habits that serve our unconscious discipleship, habits that don't fuel our narcissism but continually soften our hearts. One way of doing this is by marking time.

We mark time, umm, all the time, actually. We celebrate birthdays and anniversaries to mark the progression from our birth or our marriage or our employment. For my five-year anniversary at my company, I asked for and received a color printer that I ultimately never even took out of the box. It's sitting on top of a cabinet in my utility room; apparently I don't print in color near as much as I think I do. Even so, however, every time I open that cabinet and that box teeters on the edge, threatening to fall on my head, I'm reminded that I've worked in the same place for a long, long time.

Beyond those annual events are the more regular marked rhythms of our lives: We work on a set schedule for a fixed period of time each day; we go home when the bell rings. Our weekend is distinguished from our workweek on a predictable rhythm. We might go to church on Sundays, play basketball on Wednesdays, see friends on Fridays, do laundry on Saturdays. All of these are rhythms we've settled into in our lives. We don't think about it most days; we just go about our business.

We have similar ways of marking time with God. Some are momentous; several church traditions have time-bound sacraments such as the baptism or consecration of infants or rites of passage such as confirmation. Some friends of mine gave each of their sons a shield on his tenth birthday and a sword on his thirteenth as a way of communicating his growing responsibilities and the challenges that he will face as he grows older. That sword or shield, that baptismal certificate or confirmation Bible serves as a reminder to us over time that in our history is that moment of transition from one status to another. They continue to remind us even if we forget to wipe the dust off them, even if we've buried the photographs of the event in a shoebox somewhere, even if we're otherwise just going about our business.

There are ways of marking more common passages of time spiritually as well, however. Lynne Baab, author of *Sabbath Keeping*, suggests ways of leaning into the ancient practice of Sabbath as a time of rest and renewal. Among other suggestions in her book are blocking off every Sabbath in your day planner and lighting a particular candle at the beginning of your Sabbath observance, blowing it out again when the day is over. Bill Hybels, whose Willow Creek Community Church celebrates Communion once a month, suggests that Christians make every effort to participate in every Lord's Supper with their community of faith—to avoid travel commitments that pull them away from the event or to find a local church to serve as a surrogate if travel is unavoidable. These and other regularly repeated spiritual practices can become habitual, once you've gotten through the awkward phase of habituating yourself to them. God is doing silent work in you simply because you've gotten yourself in his way.

Of course, habits have a way of calcifying and growing stale. Thomas Merton wrote of so sacred a cow as praying Scripture that "the fact that the Psalms become a habit is certainly of little value if they become a bad habit."[17] They can also serve as bragging rights: "Oh, I had the most wonderful Sabbath observance this weekend." I remember the visceral reaction I had when I was conscripted into watching the opening episode of Oprah Winfrey's year of nurturing the soul. The sight of Oprah the great guru nestled in a giant cedar bathtub in front of a camera, broadcasting to the whole world, calling out to the great spirit of, I suppose, pampering and preening, proved too much for my theological and aesthetic sensibilities. I declined to join the church of Oprah that year.

The primary function of spiritual habits as historically practiced by Jesus, by contrast, is to get in the way of Jesus. We're not growing ourselves or nurturing our spirits so much as we're tricking ourselves into being open to the work of God in us. In that sense these habits of marking time serve to wake us up just enough that we reopen ourselves to God but not so much that we get self-conscious about it. It's the difference between being nudged in our sleep enough that we stop snoring for a few minutes, as opposed to setting our alarm for every fifteen minutes and waking up the whole apartment.

This is not a diatribe against rest: American culture has a cultic impulse that is manifested in the phrase "I'll sleep when I'm dead"—a triumphalistic mantra that suggests that I am indefatigable, that I can do whatever I set my mind to. It's even given sacred status in the notion of the "Protestant/Puritan work ethic." God certainly calls his people to rest regularly—rest is part of the rhythms that he has established for us. It's where the notion of Sabbath came from in the first place.

No, this is a rant against zombies. God didn't call us out of Me-Ville so that we could stop thinking, stop actively engaging the world he's placed us in. Like Peter and the Gentiles, we are called to think on our feet, to stay alert to where God is directing us and what we're encountering along the way. Marking time, looking for God in the midst of quiet and loud moments, getting ourselves in the way of Jesus—these make the difference between trudging aimlessly through the desert and marching expectantly toward the city of God. We know by faith that as we walk and walk and walk, our feet will not fail us and that at the far end of the journey is a home in the land our loving Father has promised us, a city where Christ is King and God our Mighty Fortress—a city worth living in forever.

• ESCAPE ROUTES •

PRAYING WITH OUR EYES OPEN

I don't know about you, but sometimes closing my eyes is the worst thing for my prayer life. To close my eyes may help me disengage with the external world—the floor that needs sweeping, the clock that keeps ticking—but often it throws back the curtain to the harsh light of my inner disquiet. Meanwhile that clock keeps ticking, and the memory of that dirty floor is still raising its own ruckus in my head.

Sometimes it seems that the easiest thing in the world is to forget what Jesus promised: "I am with you always." He stands amid the clamor and offers to help us sort the whole mess out, but the clamor has its own appeal—the opportunity to show that we can organize our own universe, that we can center ourselves, thank you very much. We don't realize until later the significance of systematically, automatically nudging Jesus out of the mundane realities of our daily life. With that in mind here are some disciplines that may offer us an occasional gentle reminder that Jesus is nudging his way in:

Quiet time
- Whenever you notice that you're alone, say a simple prayer, something like, "Speak, Lord, for your servant is listening."
- Whenever you think of it, recite a simple Scripture, like, "I am with you always, till the end of the age," to remind yourself that you're not really alone.
- Make note of the thoughts that occupy your mind. Write down the thoughts that call for action. Pray about the thoughts that you can't do anything about.

Interrupted quiet time

- When you're interrupted during time that was quiet, remember Jesus' reaction to the annoying rich young ruler: "He looked on him and loved him." Ask God for the strength to do the same in the midst of this interruption.

- Pray quickly for discernment about the nature of the interruption and your response. Sometimes you're needed to address a problem, and your decision at that point becomes whether to respond immediately, point someone in another direction, or set a time frame for your response. It could be that there's more to be done in your time alone, and the best thing to do is to get back to it.

- Sometimes, however, an interruption manifests a need for you to be immediately present to a person—maybe just to sit there in solidarity. Those interruptions may seem on the surface to be the least justifiable, but they may just as well be the most urgent. Ask God to help you see past your own need and see through the person's stated request to get a good look at the unarticulated need, and to help you respond to that.

Loud time

- Before you get together with a group of people, imagine it as a mission, and consecrate it with missional language such as Isaiah's cry, "Here I am, Lord; send me." Be careful not to set a missional agenda for the time together; just make the effort to consecrate the moment.

- Enter into group situations as though you're on a God Hunt or like you're reading through a Where's Waldo? book: *In this room full of people, where will I find God, and what will I find God doing?*

- At the end of your time together with a group of people, whether it's a formal gathering or informal get-together, offer a prayer of thanks for

the people God has surrounded you with—either alone or with some
of the people you've been with.

- Play an anonymous game of twenty questions, making a concerted effort
  to keep another person talking and to learn more about him or her.

At the end of each day consider taking inventory of your quiet times and loud
times, reflecting on how they worked together to define the day. Take stock of
what were the most meaningful moments of your day and whether you would
characterize them as quiet or loud. Then take a few moments to consider how
you might mark tomorrow's passage. Then pray, perhaps so simple a prayer
as the one so many kids have been taught to pray:

> Now I lay me down to sleep.
> I pray the Lord my soul to keep.

Then give yourself to the Lord, and sleep well.

Afterword:
YOUR KINGDOM COME

When Jesus' followers wondered how to pray, he taught them this:

> Our Father who art in heaven
> Hallowed be thy name
> Thy kingdom come, thy will be done
> On earth as it is in heaven.
>
> Give us this day our daily bread
> Forgive us our debts as we forgive our debtors.
> And lead us not into temptation
> But deliver us from evil.

Or words to that effect. It's interesting to me that although this prayer begins exclusively with prayers of reverence, giving honor to God and expressing submissiveness to his will, it then moves into prayers that are exclusively oriented around the self. We are given permission by Jesus to ask God for our daily needs, for forgiveness, for our protection, for our salvation. Me, me, me. Us, us, us. Dallas Willard calls the prayer "a vote of 'no confidence' in our own abilities. As the series of requests begins with the glorification of God, it ends with acknowledgment of the feebleness of human beings."[18] I'm reminded by the prayer Jesus taught us that God is rightly to be revered—but also that God is interested in our well-being. God wants to be honored but ensures that in giving him that honor we will not fall through the cracks.

That's a helpful reassurance for me, because I'm usually swinging like a pendulum between almost fanatical expressions of the greatness of God and almost obsessive preoccupation with myself. It's only the grace of God that slows my oscillation, settles my double-mindedness.

SHUT UP AND PRAY

The other hidden message of the Lord's Prayer is that it's a prayer affirming the grace of God. The language of prayer is a tricky business. So often we fall into patterns of asking God to endorse our actions or otherwise operate as our copilot: "God help me to make a good presentation today." "God bless this fast food which I am about to receive." The Lord's Prayer is nothing of the sort; Jesus invites us to do what Moses invited his followers to do:

> Don't be afraid. Stand firm and watch GOD do his work
> of salvation for you today…. GOD will fight the battle for
> you. And you? You keep your mouths shut! (Ex. 14:13–14)

In the first stanza of the Lord's Prayer, we give God honor, but we don't commit anything to him. Devout as it is, it's really simply stating the obvious: God's name is hallowed; his kingdom is coming; his creation will ultimately reflect his will. In the second stanza we present our requests, both negative and positive, but in passive voice: "give us

... forgive us ... lead us not ... deliver us...."

Jesus is teaching us in this prayer that even though we spend our days striving to be good, to do the right thing, ultimately our motives are so compromised by our finiteness, our limited vision, that we can't count on our actions to get us anywhere. And then Jesus whispers, by way of this prayer: "That's okay. I'm here for you. I'm making things work out for you both now and forevermore."

Sinead O'Connor wrote a song that conveys this gentle, nurturing sort of lordship, borrowing from Jesus' weeping prophecy over Jerusalem: "How long I have longed to take you in my arms as a hen with her chicks."

> Child, I'm so glad I found you
> Although my arms have always been around you.
> Sweet bird, although you did not see me
> I saw you.

Sara Groves conveyed the spirit of the prayer in a single phrase: "It's gonna be all right."

SO BE IT

I've never been more pendulum-like than when I was in college. It's understandable, I suppose; there you are, yanked out of eighteen years of normalcy and dropped unceremoniously into an environment where your convictions are what you make of them. Meanwhile, you're being taught to second-guess everything you've ever been taught. In other words, you're growing up. None of this "take you in my arms as a hen with her chicks." Welcome to four years of being kicked out of a nest.

Sometime within those four years of college I attended a very special chapel presentation. The Covenant Service was a regular feature of the ministry of the great British preacher and founder of Methodism, John Wesley. The service was offered annually on New Year's Eve in London and regularly on the circuits he rode across the English countryside as a means of helping Christians understand and renew their Christian commitments. Some two hundred years later I sat in the chapel at Illinois Wesleyan University and took part in that same service. I ate it up like it was a chocolate-covered cherry.

The highlight for me was a single line: "Let me be employed for you, or laid aside for you." I understood immediately what the line was suggesting: If God wants to do great things with me, so be it. If God wants to ignore me so he has more time and energy to do great things with someone else, so be it. I was just fanatical enough that evening that this seemed like reasonable service, a perfectly sensible commitment to make. So I honed in on that line as I prayed silently to my God: "Let me be employed for you, *or laid aside for you.*" I left that service happy and blessed.

Then, apparently, God laid me aside for a while.

At least that's how it felt. My music career wasn't taking off; my love life was inordinately perplexing, my grades weren't great, my classes weren't exciting, my friendships weren't fulfilling, and on and on. I had, to borrow from the language of commerce, "buyer's remorse." I got angry at God; I got angry at myself for striking a fool's bargain. I attempted to negotiate a settlement: "Okay, God, you can lay me aside in the music department, but help a brother out with the ladies, all right?"

To be honest, every time I perceive that things aren't going my way, my mind slips back—even if only for a minute—to that Covenant

Service when, in the throes of my inflated sense of self-righteousness, I thought I could get along just fine without God, when I thought I'd do him a favor by releasing him of any obligation to me.

Compare my smugness with the desperation of Jacob, an admittedly ethically compromised patriarch of God's people. When he encountered God, he didn't lean back, cross his arms, and say, "Don't sweat it, God; I'm good." He wrestled God to the ground and refused to let go until God blessed him. That wrestling match came at its own cost: Jacob walked with a limp from that day forward. But that limp reminded him that the God he worshipped was both powerful enough to wound him and loving enough to bless him.

I still think back often to that Covenant Service, even on my more level-headed days. I think back to it because regardless of how foolish I was that day, God was good. He was good to me in the same way that he was good to Peter when Peter foolishly told Jesus not to suffer for him, when Peter foolishly declared himself seaworthy and faithful enough to walk on water at the Lord's command, when Peter foolishly refused to let Jesus wash his feet and then foolishly tried to save face by demanding a full-body wash, when Peter foolishly followed Jesus to the temple only to deny that they were friends. God loves the foolish as much as he loves the wise, so we might as well admit when we've been foolish and enjoy a good laugh about it every now and then.

I know now, with the passage of time, that my prayer of self-sufficiency that day didn't negate God's prior covenant promise: "I will never leave you nor forsake you." God didn't come all the way from his kingdom to Me-Ville to get me simply to part ways with me; God wants me—and with me, you and really all of us—to be in his kingdom, which is where he is, which as the Lord's Prayer suggests, is on earth even as it is in heaven.

⋅ ESCAPE ROUTES ⋅

DELIVER US FROM ME-VILLE

I leave you with an extended passage from John Wesley's Covenant Service, not so you can make the same foolish promise I made but so you can see that despite our folly God is levelheaded, knowing us as fully as he loves us. Let this Covenant prayer affirm that Jesus is above all our Covenant friend, delivering us from Me-Ville and leading us along the rough and rocky path to a sure destination at the throne of God.

Christ has many services to be done.
Some are more easy and honorable,
Others are more difficult and disgraceful.
Some are suitable to our inclinations and interests,
Others are contrary to both.
In some we may please Christ and please ourselves.
But then there are other works where we cannot please Christ
Except by denying ourselves.
It is necessary, therefore,
That we consider what it means to be a servant of Christ.
Let us, therefore, go to Christ, and pray:

Let me be your servant, under your command.
I will no longer be my own.
I will give up myself to your will in all things.

Be satisfied that Christ shall give you your place and work.

Lord, make me what you will.

I put myself fully into your hands:

Put me to doing, put me to suffering,

Let me be employed for you, or laid aside for you,

Let me be full, let me be empty,

Let me have all things, let me have nothing.

I freely and with a willing heart give it all to your pleasure and disposal....

You have dedicated yourself to God.

With God's power, never go back....

O mighty God, the Lord Omnipotent, Father, Son, and Holy Spirit,

You have now become my Covenant Friend.

And I, through your infinite grace, have become your covenant servant.

So be it.

ROAD MAPS

Somewhere along the way, as you indulge yourself in writing a book, you experience a revelation that knocks you off your high horse: There's more to be said, and you don't have the wherewithal to say it.

That epiphany came early in the process for me, and it kept reminding me of itself with every paragraph I wrote, every sentence I rewrote. Fortunately I'm blessed with good friends with good libraries, and so I've along the way been turned on to some great resources that will reward your own further consideration of Me-Ville and your escape from it. Some of these books are no longer in print but could be found at libraries, used-book stores, or online book outlets. If you have other ideas of what I or your fellow readers should know about, contact me at loud-time.com or at the *Deliver Us from Me-Ville* page at Facebook. I'd love to hear from you.

Each of the following books is a tough read, but each is unbelievably rewarding in its contribution to a growing discipleship and the vision it puts forward of the life in the kingdom we're called to in Christ.

- Vanier, Jean. *Becoming Human.* New York: Paulist Press, 1998.
- Wright, N. T. *The Challenge of Jesus.* Downers Grove, IL: InterVarsity Press, 1999.
- *The Confessions of St. Augustine.*
- Bonhoeffer, Dietrich. *The Cost of Discipleship.* New York: Touchstone, 1995.
- Willard, Dallas. *The Divine Conspiracy.* San Francisco:

HarperSanFrancisco, 1998.

- Mahan, Brian. *Forgetting Ourselves on Purpose.* San Francisco: Jossey-Bass, 2002.
- Benner, David. *The Gift of Being Yourself.* Downers Grove, IL: InterVarsity Press, 2002.
- Kempis, Thomas à. *The Imitation of Christ.*
- Tozer, A. W. *The Knowledge of the Holy.* San Francisco: HarperSanFrancisco, 1978.
- Bonhoeffer, Dietrich. *Life Together.* San Franscisco: HarperSanFrancisco, 1993.
- Merton, Thomas. *New Seeds of Contemplation.* New York: New Directions Book, 2007.
- Chesterton, G. K. *Orthodoxy.* Fairfield, IA: 1st World Library – Literary Society, 2007.
- Manning, Brennan. *The Ragamuffin Gospel.* Sisters, OR: Multnomah Publishers, 2000.
- Nouwen, Henri J. M. *The Return of the Prodigal Son.* New York: Continuum, 1995.
- Merton, Thomas. *Seven Storey Mountain.* New York: Harcourt Brace, 1998.
- Willard, Dallas. *The Spirit of the Disciplines.* New York: HarperCollins, 1983.

ACKNOWLEDGMENTS

What kind of nuanced nincompoop would have the sheer moxie to write a whole book on self-absorption? This kind of nuanced nincompoop, I guess. I recognized from the beginning of this process the absurdity of declaring myself an expert on narcissism, but I really, really wanted to write the book nonetheless. The following people helped me to do so without sounding absurdly absurd, and I offer them my thanks.

First off, to Margaret Feinberg, who is far too accommodating to my professional badgering and thinly veiled neuroses. I very privately asked her for advice, and she very wisely recognized that I was in fact asking for encouragement, which she has offered me throughout the publication process. Read everything Margaret writes, because it's always gracious, insightful, and delightful, much like herself.

I turned from Margaret to Don Pape, who at the time was an agent, but before I could ask him to be my agent became the publisher of trade books for David C. Cook. So I asked him instead to be my publisher. He was incredibly supportive—I think Cook has a policy about using exclamation points in e-mails—when he very easily (and somewhat legitimately) could have been incredibly discouraging. Because of Don, I now have a wonderful relationship with a company full of good people.

One of those people is Andrea Christian, my editor. I met Andrea only a few weeks before submitting my proposal to Don; we talked editor to editor rather than editor to would-be author and (to my mind, at least) had a great time doing it. Andrea is wildly professional and impressively gracious in a field where, in my experience at least, both virtues are difficult to sustain. Another of those people is Jaci Schneider, who copyedited the book with great professional aplomb, carefully excising every error of fact, infelicity of grammar or spelling, and generally every lingering embarrassment of authorial incompetence. Some of them I'm sure I put back into the book, along with a few new ones; sorry for that, Jaci. My thanks also to Kate Amaya, Amy Quicksall, Ingrid Beck, and all the other folks at David C. Cook who have been so attentive and supportive along the way to publication.

Writing anything for publication is a nerve-racking endeavor, and particularly in the case of this book, I felt highly vulnerable. What heresies would I unwittingly endorse? What ignorance would I unknowingly reveal? Where, for that matter, am I slipping into my own self-absorbed self-promotion without being aware of it? A few trustworthy friends read my first draft and gave me critical feedback that was as useful as it was charitable. Andy Crouch, Sean Gladding, Mike King, Heather Zempel, Don Everts, Brian Mahan—these are a few of my favorite people.

Also wonderfully supportive has been the Pattison family. Stewart—a great thinker and very busy pastor—nevertheless set aside time to read and comment on the book, giving me a good mix of critical feedback and pastoral guidance. Bonnie the theologian was persistently encouraging when I needed to hear theological encouragement and made very helpful suggestions of how the book might best serve the church. I'm fortunate to be a part of the congregation that they call home. Others at my church have served as very helpful sounding boards and strategists, among them my confirmation buddies Ryan, Paul, and Lauren, Dave Micksch, Ken and Bert Flisak, Bill and Pat Arnott, and Mike, Gail, and Ethan Casey.

I'm a book editor by trade, which means that I'm regularly working with authors on their books. I must here apologize to several great thinkers and writers for blathering on about Me-Ville when we should have been discussing their books: Tamara Park, Chris Heuertz, Matt Rogers, Jason Santos, Kimberlee Conway Ireton—write like the wind! Your audience eagerly awaits.

I'd also like to extend my thanks to my colleagues at InterVarsity Press, who published my first book and who have been very supportive of this second book even though it's being published by a rival company. One of the great tributes to the Christian publishing industry in America is that even at their most competitive, as companies in a capitalist economy are wont to be, relationships between companies are highly collegial. I'm thankful for the integrity and kindness of the people who populate both InterVarsity Press and David C. Cook; without them I'd be bookless, jobless, and virtually friendless.

My parents, siblings, in-laws, and extended family are a constant encouragement even when they find themselves referenced in my writing, even when they have to correct my errant memory and contend with my self-serving storytelling on a regular basis. I owe each and all a great debt. My wife in particular has indulged my interest in writing by giving me time and space and a budget to do it and the perfect mix of critique and effusion; I'm thankful for her love and kindness.

Finally my dad has throughout his life modeled for me (perhaps unknowingly) a savvy self-awareness that rarely slips into self-absorption. He maintains a sense of humor about himself and the world that regularly gives him special insight into why people do what they do and compassion for them even when they drive him crazy, nicely accomplishing the calling identified by Thomas Merton in his *Secular Journals:* "to live as a member of a human race which is no more (and no less) ridiculous than myself." This book is dedicated to him with my thanks.

◆

**May God in his mercy lead us through these times,
but above all, may he lead us to himself.**

—DIETRICH BONHOEFFER, *LETTERS AND PAPERS FROM PRISON*

◆

NOTES

CHAPTER 1

1 Mark Twain, "Autobiography of Eve," in *The Bible according to Mark Twain,* ed. Howard G. Baetzhold and Joseph B. McCullough (New York: Touchstone, 1995), 45.

2 Jean Twenge, *Generation Me: Why Today's Young Americans Are More Confident, Assertive, Entitled—and More Miserable Than Ever Before* (New York: Free Press, 2006), 52–53.

3 I'm not a psychologist, and consequently I'm no expert on why people injure themselves. My own conversations with people who self-injure have led me to think that punishment is at least a possible motivator, along with perhaps the desire to assert some control over what seems to be an out-of-control situation. But it's an unbelievably complex question and far, far beyond the scope of this book.

4 Twenge, *Generation Me,* 36.

5 Ibid., 138–39.

6 Portico Research Group, quoted in Sarah Cunningham, *Dear Church* (Grand Rapids, MI: Zondervan, 2006), 42.

7 Christopher Lasch, *The Culture of Narcissism* (New York: Norton, 1979), 60.

8 Terry Cooper, *Sin, Pride & Self-Acceptance* (Downers Grove, IL: InterVarsity Press, 2003), 143.

9 A. W. Tozer, *The Knowledge of the Holy* (San Francisco: HarperSanFrancisco, 1978), 29.

10 Cooper, *Sin, Pride & Self-Acceptance,* 17.

11 Tozer, *Knowledge of the Holy,* 31.

CHAPTER 2

1 "Me Worship," http://www.youtube.com/watch?v=t9dvVp0Nxjo. Accessed February 25, 2007.

2 Lasch, *Culture of Narcissism,* 43–44.

3 Andy Crouch, seminar at Catalyst Labs, Atlanta, Georgia, October 2006. I'm paraphrasing from sketchy notes, but this is the gist of the illustration Andy offered. My apologies if I've made him sound any less articulate and brilliant than he actually is.

4 Our neighbor gave us the snowblower when she retired to the Deep South; I'm glad we invited her over!

5 Merton, Thomas, *The Secular Journal* New York: Farrar, Strauss and Giroux, 1959

6 Lasch, *Culture of Narcissism,* 65.

7 Jean Vanier, *Becoming Human* (New York: Paulist Press, 1998), 80.

8 Dietrich Bonhoeffer, *Christ the Center,* vol. 3 (San Francisco: Harper-

SanFrancisco, 1978), 35.

9 A friend who read an early draft of this book suggested that pro-me is better translated as "in the place of on behalf of." His translation, I freely admit, is more precise than mine, but let me quickly add that my translation is much funnier than his.

10 Thomas Merton, *New Seeds of Contemplation* (New York: New Directions, 1961), 37.

11 John Cotton, quoted in Lasch, *Culture of Narcissism*, 54. Apparently in the seventeenth century, Puritans didn't know how to spell.

12 Bonhoeffer, *Christ the Center*, p. 47.

13 Here I borrow language from Derek Webb in the Caedmon's Call song "Standing Up for Nothing," which just so happens to be playing as I type. Weird.

14 A friend of mine read this and suggested that perhaps, as we walk through our neighborhoods, we should pray about whether God wants us living somewhere else—in a more culturally diverse setting, in a place where we will be more consistently confronted with the realities of injustice, maybe even in a country that's unfamiliar with Jesus. But that's just crazy talk.

CHAPTER 3

1 Gas station attendants still pump your gas for you in some parts of the country. Apparently they're required to by law there. I don't go to those places, but I'm sure they're very nice, very accommodating people.

2 The "Zimmerman" referenced in this song is Bob Dylan, but I like to think Lennon had me in mind. That doesn't make me a shallow person, does it?

3 Dietrich Bonhoeffer, *The Cost of Discipleship* (New York: Touchstone, 1995).

4 Bonhoeffer, *Christ the Center*, 60–61.

5 Bonhoeffer, *Cost of Discipleship*.

6 Bonhoeffer, *Christ the Center*, 38.

7 Thomas Merton, *Praying the Psalms* (Collegeville, MN: Liturgical Press, 1956), 9.

8 David Nimmer, music notes to the performance of Biblical Songs nos. 4 ("God Is My Shepherd") and 8 ("Turn Thee to Me") by Anton Dvorak, at Community Presbyterian Church, Lombard, IL, August 26, 2007.

CHAPTER 4

1 Bonhoeffer, *Cost of Discipleship*, 58.

2 Brian Mahan, *Forgetting Ourselves on Purpose* (San Francisco: Jossey-Bass, 2002), 158.

3 Bonhoeffer, *Cost of Discipleship*, 164.

4 Quoted in Andy Le Peau and Linda Doll, *Heart. Soul. Mind. Strength.* (Downers Grove, IL: InterVarsity Press, 2006), 19.

5 Vanier, *Becoming Human*, 35–36.

6 Merton, quoted in Nouwen, *Thomas Merton: Contemplative Critic,* (New York: Triumph Books, 1991), 44.

7 My own personal take on this passage, reached entirely unscientifically, is that John did live to see Jesus come again, in a vision that John was taken up into, articulated in the book of Revelation. That may be what Jesus meant, but then again it may not: In either case, it really was none of Peter's business. Nor is it my business or yours, so back off.

8 Dietrich Bonhoeffer, *Life Together* (San Francisco: HarperSanFrancisco, 1954), 23–24.

9 Dallas Willard, *The Divine Conspiracy* (San Francisco: HarperSanFrancisco, 1998), 236.

10 Bonhoeffer, *Cost of Discipleship,* 158–59.

11 Ibid., 44.

12 I'm grateful to Sean Gladding and his fellow teachers at Mercy Street, Houston, for their series "Ten" about the exodus, which can at this writing be downloaded at www.mercy-street.org.

13 Merton, quoted in Nouwen, *Thomas Merton: Contemplative Critic,* 120.

14 Merton, *New Seeds of Contemplation,* quoted in James Martin, *Becoming Who You Are* (Mahwah, NJ: Hidden Spring, 2006), ix.

15 Mahan, *Forgetting Ourselves on Purpose,* 90–91. Because Mahan's brilliant insights into the human condition are so nicely supplemented by his punchy prose and clever wit, I like to call this "nature's most nearly perfect book."

16 It's unlike everything else in that it was founded and is sustained by the

God of the universe, but that's another story.

17 Mahan, *Forgetting Ourselves on Purpose,* 120.

18 I first encountered the phrase *agere contra* in the writings of James Martin, but I think I lived it growing up Roman Catholic; when I first read of the concept I had a profound sense of "Well yeah, of course," before ultimately suspecting that *agere contra* is part of the script handed down to me.

19 Martin, *Becoming Who You Are,* 34.

20 Vanier, *Becoming Human,* 15–16.

21 Merton, *New Seeds of Contemplation,* 49–50.

22 For a good discussion of how churches can be authentic witnessing communities, read Brian Sanders' *Life after Church: God's Call to Disillusioned Christians* (Downers Grove, IL: InterVarsity Press, 2007).

CHAPTER 5

1 By writing this, I don't mean to suggest that John or any other writer of Scripture manipulated the truth; I suspect that John actually did outrun Peter and that Jesus actually did love John dearly. I only suggest that what struck each writer as particularly important had to do intimately with who he was and, I daresay, serves part of the function of inspiration. So John's gospel will recall details that are particularly important to John, entrusting those details particularly important to Peter to another writer.

2 Bonhoeffer, *Cost of Discipleship,* 100.

3 Vanier, *Becoming Human,* 71.

4 Mahan, *Forgetting Ourselves on Purpose,* 109–12.

5 Merton, quoted in Nouwen, *Thomas Merton: Contemplative Critic,* 135.

6 Vanier, *Becoming Human,* 7.

7 Bonhoeffer, *Life Together,* 26–27.

8 Ibid., 30.

9 Merton, quoted in Nouwen, *Thomas Merton: Contemplative Critic,* 33.

10 Bonhoeffer, *Life Together,* 32–36.

11 Merton, *New Seeds of Contemplation,* 48.

12 If I were her husband and had started a Ramones tribute band, I would
have called it "Teenage Phlebotomy." But "Gabba Gabba Hey" is a cool
name too.

13 My friend Joel Scandrett wrote a very brief theology of blood donation
that I posted on my Web site, loud-time.com. You can read it in the
archives for summer 2007.

14 Nouwen, quoted in Martin, *Becoming Who You Are,* 51.

15 Vanier, *Becoming Human,* 28.

16 Bonhoeffer, *Life Together,* 77.

17 Mahan, *Forgetting Ourselves on Purpose,* 161.

18 I don't mean by this that we don't need to become good. Goodness is
a virtue we should of course pursue, but confession has a more profound
potential than simply forcing us to say out loud what we've done wrong;
it's a forum for becoming appropriately disillusioned with ourselves.

19 Dietrich Bonhoeffer, *Letters and Papers from Prison* (San Francisco: Harper, 1960), 158–59, emphasis added.

CHAPTER 6

1 For a delightfully trippy exploration of the mystery of God's sovereign presence in the world, read G. K. Chesterton's *The Man Who Was Thursday.* It's pretty old-school British, but it's worth it.

2 Bonhoeffer, *Cost of Discipleship,* 88.

3 Merton, quoted in Nouwen, *Thomas Merton: Contemplative Critic,* 141.

4 Willard, *Divine Conspiracy,* 41.

5 A friend who read the book noted, very insightfully, that in this encounter Jesus once again shows himself as *pro-me:* "What Jesus does on the beach is beautiful: He not only lets Peter know that he is 'for Peter'—he also lets Peter hear himself say three times that he is 'for Jesus.'"

6 Karen Mains, *The God Hunt* (Downers Grove, IL: InterVarsity Press, 2003), 13.

7 John Ortberg, *God Is Closer Than You Think* (Grand Rapids, MI: Zondervan, 2005), 91.

8 The author was the eminently quotable Søren Kierkegaard, who became immediately interesting to me for that very reason—along with the funky slash through the "o" in his first name.

9 Comedian Jim Gaffigan sees the humor in the challenge Moses faced

telling others about his private audience with God: "Umm, Moses, we think you've been burning some bush."

10 I read this quotation from Carl Jung, I freely admit, in a catalog of Christmas gifts for smart people. I didn't buy it, and Carl Jung would not have called himself a Christian, but you have to admit, it's a pretty nice quote.

11 A. W. Tozer, *Knowledge of the Holy,* 76.

12 Frederick Buechner, *Now and Then* (San Francisco: Harper & Row, 1983), 92, 87, reprinted in *Listening to Your Life* (San Francisco: Harper-SanFrancisco, 1992), 2.

13 Bonhoeffer, *Christ the Center,* 50.

14 Vince Bacote, a professor at Wheaton College, made this offhand comment during a class offered at our church.

15 Merton, quoted in Nouwen, *Thomas Merton: Contemplative Critic,* 128.

16 Ibid., 67.

17 Merton, *Praying the Psalms,* 21.

18 Willard, *Divine Conspiracy,* 265.

DELIVER US FROM ME-VILLE DISCUSSION GUIDE

1 The Deadly Sin of Self-Absorption

2 The Genesis of Superbia

3 The Fall into Me-Ville

4 Any God Worth His Salt

5 The One Thing Is Everything

6 In God's Orbit

7 Artifacts of the Kingdom of Self

8 The Blessings of Discomfort

9 So Many Sets of Footprints in the Sand

10 If God Says It's Okay

11 Our Covenant Friend

1: THE DEADLY SIN OF SELF-ABSORPTION

FROM THE INTRODUCTION TO DELIVER US FROM ME-VILLE

Superbia [self-absorption, narcissism] is one of the seven deadly sins not just because it has the capacity to be calamitous, as in the case of Peter, but because it can be so common, as in the case of myself. Self-absorption is a besetting sin among all God's children, nipping at the church's heels throughout its history, and as such it must be met by the vigilance of the people of God to hold it at bay.

1. List some examples of self-absorption you've recently observed in contemporary culture.

2. The author caught himself growing increasingly proud of himself while portraying the disciple Peter in a play about Jesus. Read Matthew 16:13–26.

    When Jesus arrived in the villages of Caesarea Philippi, he asked his disciples, "What are people saying about who the Son of Man is?"
    They replied, "Some think he is John the Baptizer, some say Elijah, some Jeremiah or one of the other prophets."
    He pressed them, "And how about you? Who do you say I am?"
    Simon Peter said, "You're the Christ, the Messiah, the

Son of the living God."

Jesus came back, "God bless you, Simon, son of Jonah! You didn't get that answer out of books or from teachers. My Father in heaven, God himself, let you in on this secret of who I really am. And now I'm going to tell you who you are, really are. You are Peter, a rock. This is the rock on which I will put together my church, a church so expansive with energy that not even the gates of hell will be able to keep it out.

"And that's not all. You will have complete and free access to God's kingdom, keys to open any and every door: no more barriers between heaven and earth, earth and heaven. A yes on earth is yes in heaven. A no on earth is no in heaven."

He swore the disciples to secrecy. He made them promise they would tell no one that he was the Messiah.

Then Jesus made it clear to his disciples that it was now necessary for him to go to Jerusalem, submit to an ordeal of suffering at the hands of the religious leaders, be killed, and then on the third day be raised up alive. Peter took him in hand, protesting, "Impossible, Master! That can never be!"

But Jesus didn't swerve. "Peter, get out of my way. Satan, get lost. You have no idea how God works."

Then Jesus went to work on his disciples. "Anyone who intends to come with me has to let me lead. You're not in the driver's seat; I am. Don't run from suffering; embrace it. Follow me and I'll show you how. Self-help is no help at all. Self-sacrifice is the way, my way, to finding yourself, your true self. What kind of deal is it to get everything you want but lose yourself? What could you ever trade your soul for?"

In what ways might Peter be considered prideful in this passage?

3. What advice does Jesus give his followers about self-absorption here?

4. What kind of damage can self-absorption do to a church?

There's the kingdom that God reigns over, and there's the kingdom that we assert in our everyday lives. They're commingled in the way that the city of Chicago and its suburbs, for example, are commingled. The suburbs thrive at least in part because of their proximity to the city, but they would never dream of allowing Chicago's mayor to tell them what to do. The suburbs fancy themselves distinct from the city, surrounding it and keeping it contained; meanwhile, in the thrust of history Chicago keeps growing and expanding and asserting its influence.

5. The author suggests that people benefit from and even associate themselves with God in their everyday lives but simultaneously live as independently from God as possible. How do you see that play out in contemporary culture?

6. What are some areas of your life that you could open up to God more?

7. What are you hoping to get out of reading and discussing *Deliver Us from Me-Ville*?

2: THE GENESIS OF SUPERBIA

FROM CHAPTER ONE: THE HIGH COST OF LIVING IN ME-VILLE

Human beings are important because they are made in the image of God and bear a responsibility, in keeping with their divine likeness, to the kingdom of God.

The danger comes when small children, or grown adults, say "I'm important, yo!" over and over and over again. Somewhere in that repetition their sense of significance morphs into something more sinister: self-importance. Welcome to Me-Ville.

1. What's the difference, in your mind, between self-esteem and self-importance?

2. Read Genesis 1:26-31.

> God spoke: "Let us make human beings in our image,
>   make them
>   reflecting our nature
>   So they can be responsible for the fish in the sea,
>   the birds in the air, the cattle,
>   And, yes, Earth itself,
>   and every animal that moves on the face of Earth."
> God created human beings;
>   he created them godlike,

Reflecting God's nature.

He created them male and female.

God blessed them:

"Prosper! Reproduce! Fill Earth! Take charge!

Be responsible for fish in the sea and birds in the
air,

for every living thing that moves on the face of
Earth."

Then God said, "I've given you

every sort of seed-bearing plant on Earth

And every kind of fruit-bearing tree,

given them to you for food.

To all animals and all birds,

everything that moves and breathes,

I give whatever grows out of the ground for food."

And there it was.

God looked over everything he had made;

it was so good, so very good!

How does God describe human beings at the moment of their
creation?

3. What did God tell Adam and Eve to do? How important do you
think they felt in that moment?

4. What did God promise to Adam and Eve in verses 29–30? In
your mind, was this a good gig or a bad deal? Why?

5. Read Genesis 3:6–13.

> When the Woman saw that the tree looked like good eat-
> ing and realized what she would get out of it—she'd know
> everything!—she took and ate the fruit and then gave some
> to her husband, and he ate.
>
> Immediately the two of them did "see what's really going
> on"—saw themselves naked! They sewed fig leaves together as
> makeshift clothes for themselves.
>
> When they heard the sound of GOD strolling in the gar-
> den in the evening breeze, the Man and his Wife hid in the
> trees of the garden, hid from GOD.
>
> GOD called to the Man: "Where are you?"
>
> He said, "I heard you in the garden and I was afraid
> because I was naked. And I hid."
>
> GOD said, "Who told you you were naked? Did you eat
> from that tree I told you not to eat from?"
>
> The Man said, "The Woman you gave me as a compan-
> ion, she gave me fruit from the tree, and, yes, I ate it."
>
> GOD said to the Woman, "What is this that you've
> done?"
>
> "The serpent seduced me," she said, "and I ate."

Why did Adam and Eve hide from God?

6. The author mentions the contemporary problem of people
   "externalizing" their moral breaches. In what ways do you see this
   happening with Adam and Eve? Where do you see it in contemporary culture?

7. Why do you think the early church found *superbia* so dangerous? What concerns you about self-absorption today?

3: THE FALL INTO ME-VILLE

FROM CHAPTER ONE: THE HIGH COST OF LIVING IN ME-VILLE

I was rewriting the story I found myself in so that I could play a better part. It's a helpful coping mechanism: Allies become enemies, heroes become bit players, heroines become damsels in distress, all in the service of our placing ourselves in the center—whether we're really hero quality or not.

1. In what settings are you tempted to make yourself the hero?

2. If you had, like the author, embarrassed yourself in front of a roomful of important people on an important day for you, how would you have reacted? How would you have redeemed yourself?

3. Read Genesis 11:1–9.

> At one time, the whole Earth spoke the same language. It so happened that as they moved out of the east, they came upon a plain in the land of Shinar and settled down.
> They said to one another, "Come, let's make bricks and fire them well." They used brick for stone and tar for mortar.
> Then they said, "Come, let's build ourselves a city and a tower that reaches Heaven. Let's make ourselves famous so we won't be scattered here and there across the Earth."

GOD came down to look over the city and the tower those people had built.

GOD took one look and said, "One people, one language; why, this is only a first step. No telling what they'll come up with next—they'll stop at nothing! Come, we'll go down and garble their speech so they won't understand each other." Then GOD scattered them from there all over the world. And they had to quit building the city. That's how it came to be called Babel, because there GOD turned their language into "babble." From there GOD scattered them all over the world.

What's unusual about the desire here to be "famous"?

4. How do you make sense of God's response? Was it for his benefit or theirs?

5. What causes people like William Hung to set themselves up for humiliation?

6. Whose response to Hung's performance was more appropriate: Simon Cowell's ("You can't sing; you can't dance") or Paula Abdul's ("You're the best!")? Why?

7. Did you try out the escape routes at the end of chapter one? If you did, what was the experience like for you? If you didn't, which questions are you most intrigued by? Why?

4: ANY GOD WORTH HIS SALT

FROM CHAPTER TWO: JESUS VISITS US IN ME-VILLE

We gladly approach the God of Me-Ville in worship because he can't be bothered to approach us in rebuke. Meanwhile the God of the Bible, wrapped in unapproachable light, lies outside the boundaries of Me-Ville, outside our field of vision.

1. How do you think God is generally perceived by people in our culture today? Is God thought of more commonly as near to us or far off?

2. Is it easier for you to think of God as inapproachable or accessible? Why?

If Jesus came to my world, I expect he would discover that I, like the rest of the world, "didn't even notice ... didn't want him" (John 1:9–10). Once we had made the proper introductions, of course, I might feel differently, probably conflicted. On the one hand, this guest is important; this guest improves my social standing. To have the Son of God in my home tells the world that I am important, yo, that my home is sacred.

Of course, I've already decided that my home is sacred, so to the degree that Jesus enters my home and exposes it to the judgment of a holy God, he becomes an immediate threat. He's no longer watching from a distance, like the grandfatherly God I've come to appreciate; he's now in my face.

3. Read Luke 5:1–11.

Once when he was standing on the shore of Lake Gennesaret, the crowd was pushing in on him to better hear the Word of God. He noticed two boats tied up. The fishermen had just left them and were out scrubbing their nets. He climbed into the boat that was Simon's and asked him to put out a little from the shore. Sitting there, using the boat for a pulpit, he taught the crowd.

When he finished teaching, he said to Simon, "Push out into deep water and let your nets out for a catch."

Simon said, "Master, we've been fishing hard all night and haven't caught even a minnow. But if you say so, I'll let out the nets." It was no sooner said than done—a huge haul of fish, straining the nets past capacity. They waved to their partners in the other boat to come help them. They filled both boats, nearly swamping them with the catch.

Simon Peter, when he saw it, fell to his knees before Jesus. "Master, leave. I'm a sinner and can't handle this holiness. Leave me to myself." When they pulled in that catch of fish, awe overwhelmed Simon and everyone with him. It was the same with James and John, Zebedee's sons, coworkers with Simon.

Jesus said to Simon, "There is nothing to fear. From now on you'll be fishing for men and women." They pulled their boats up on the beach, left them, nets and all, and followed him.

In what ways does Peter resist Jesus here? In what ways is he receptive to Jesus?

4. How does Jesus show in this encounter that he wants what's best for Peter?

5. What are the advantages of a God who does not remain far off? What new challenges does that present?

6. If Jesus were to invade your space today, how might he challenge your faith? What nets would you have to drop to follow him?

7. Did you try this chapter's escape routes? What was it like for you? If not, which part intrigues you the most? Why?

5: THE ONE THING IS EVERYTHING

FROM CHAPTER THREE: JESUS DISPLACES US

Regardless of how competent I am to attend to the overwhelming events of my life, regardless of how deep a hole I find myself in, ultimately in Me-Ville I will face such challenges alone.

1. What makes people reluctant to give advice?

2. How has Jesus served as a guide or counselor for you?

3. Why might people be reluctant to submit to guidance from Jesus?

4. Read Mark 10:13–31.

The people brought children to Jesus, hoping he might touch them. The disciples shooed them off. But Jesus was irate and let them know it: "Don't push these children away. Don't ever get between them and me. These children are at the very center of life in the kingdom. Mark this: Unless you accept God's kingdom in the simplicity of a child, you'll never get in." Then, gathering the children up in his arms, he laid his hands of blessing on them.

As he went out into the street, a man came running up,

greeted him with great reverence, and asked, "Good Teacher, what must I do to get eternal life?"

Jesus said, "Why are you calling me good? No one is good, only God. You know the commandments: Don't murder, don't commit adultery, don't steal, don't lie, don't cheat, honor your father and mother."

He said, "Teacher, I have—from my youth—kept them all!"

Jesus looked him hard in the eye—and loved him! He said, "There's one thing left: Go sell whatever you own and give it to the poor. All your wealth will then be heavenly wealth. And come follow me."

The man's face clouded over. This was the last thing he expected to hear, and he walked off with a heavy heart. He was holding on tight to a lot of things, and not about to let go.

Looking at his disciples, Jesus said, "Do you have any idea how difficult it is for people who 'have it all' to enter God's kingdom?" The disciples couldn't believe what they were hearing, but Jesus kept on: "You can't imagine how difficult. I'd say it's easier for a camel to go through a needle's eye than for the rich to get into God's kingdom."

That set the disciples back on their heels. "Then who has any chance at all?" they asked.

Jesus was blunt: "No chance at all if you think you can pull it off by yourself. Every chance in the world if you let God do it."

Peter tried another angle: "We left everything and followed you."

Jesus said, "Mark my words, no one who sacrifices house, brothers, sisters, mother, father, children, land—whatever—because of me and the Message will lose out. They'll get it all back, but multiplied many times in homes, brothers, sisters, mothers, children, and land—but also in troubles. And then the bonus of eternal life! This is once again the Great Reversal: Many who are first will end up last, and the last first."

In what ways does Jesus relate differently to the little children, the rich young ruler, and the disciples?

We don't just need to think differently if we want to break out of the prison that Me-Ville has become; . . . we need to live differently. And Jesus says to the rich young ruler what he says to us: "Store up treasures in heaven"—get right with God, not with this faulty system you find yourself trapped in—"then come, follow me."

5. What presumptions does Jesus confront in the rich young ruler's understanding about God?

6. What does the rich young ruler have to give up to get what he wants? What does he have to take on for himself?

7. Talk about ways Jesus has displaced (or might displace) you from Me-Ville. What do you think Jesus has in mind for you next?

6: IN GOD'S ORBIT

FROM CHAPTER THREE: JESUS DISPLACES US

We do well to remember that Jesus gave up plenty not just on his way to the cross but, as Philippians 2 reminds us, on his way to the earth. By taking on flesh, Jesus lays aside the privileges of dwelling in unapproachable light. By making his ministry contingent on the faith of his hearers, Jesus forgoes the power available to him by divine right. By proclaiming the kingdom of God, Jesus subjects himself to the mockery and persecution of competing kingdoms. Jesus is already displaced when first we meet him, and he's inviting us into his displacement, which is undeniably an awkward invitation. "When Christ calls a man," Bonhoeffer puts it, "he bids him come and die."

1. What sorts of things have you felt obligated to give up as an expression of your faith? Why did you feel such obligation?

2. Read Philippians 2:1–11.

If you've gotten anything at all out of following Christ, if his love has made any difference in your life, if being in a community of the Spirit means anything to you, if you have a heart, if you care— then do me a favor: Agree with each other, love each other, be deep-spirited friends. Don't push

your way to the front; don't sweet-talk your way to the top.
Put yourself aside, and help others get ahead. Don't be
obsessed with getting your own advantage. Forget yourselves
long enough to lend a helping hand.

Think of yourselves the way Christ Jesus thought of himself. He had equal status with God but didn't think so much
of himself that he had to cling to the advantages of that status no matter what. Not at all. When the time came, he set
aside the privileges of deity and took on the status of a slave,
became human! Having become human, he stayed human. It
was an incredibly humbling process. He didn't claim special
privileges. Instead, he lived a selfless, obedient life and then
died a selfless, obedient death—and the worst kind of death
at that—a crucifixion.

Because of that obedience, God lifted him high and honored him far beyond anyone or anything, ever, so that all
created beings in heaven and on earth—even those long ago
dead and buried—will bow in worship before this Jesus
Christ, and call out in praise that he is the Master of all, to
the glorious honor of God the Father.

What is Paul requiring the Philippian church to give up? What is
he requiring them to take on?

3. In what ways does Paul's description of Jesus here encourage you
   in the displacement you've felt from your previous way of life? In
   what ways does it challenge you?

4. How has Christian faith proved to be a struggle for you?

We struggle with the temptations and frustrations of life in Me-Ville not only alongside our contemporaries but with a great cloud of witnesses throughout history. What we're experiencing is nothing new. And yet what frustrates us, what tempts us, is verified as tempting and frustrating by the witness of history, by the witness of Christ. As Jesus displaces us and takes his proper place, we get the right perspective to truly understand who we are and what comes next.

5. In what ways has a relationship with Jesus made greater sense of your life?

6. Read Psalm 40:16–17.

> But all who are hunting for you—
>   oh, let them sing and be happy.
> Let those who know what you're all about
>   tell the world you're great and not quitting.
> And me? I'm a mess. I'm nothing and have nothing:
>   make something of me.
> You can do it; you've got what it takes—
>   but God, don't put it off.

In what ways has following God led you to "sing and be happy"?

7. What do you hope God will make of you as you allow Jesus to be at your center?

7: ARTIFACTS OF THE KINGDOM OF SELF

FROM CHAPTER FOUR: JESUS DELIVERS US

Not only we, but whole systems that have been manufactured around us, have their origins in this discipline of self-assertion, of self-preservation. They're artifacts of the kingdom of self. As such, they are not okay; they're replete with defects. Meanwhile Jesus is doing his magic.

1. Where in your everyday life do you feel pressure to conform to the values of Me-Ville?

2. Read Matthew 17:24–27.

> When they arrived at Capernaum, the tax men came to Peter and asked, "Does your teacher pay taxes?"
> Peter said, "Of course."
> But as soon as they were in the house, Jesus confronted him. "Simon, what do you think? When a king levies taxes, who pays—his children or his subjects?"
> He answered, "His subjects."
> Jesus said, "Then the children get off free, right? But so we don't upset them needlessly, go down to the lake, cast a hook, and pull in the first fish that bites. Open its mouth and you'll find a coin. Take it and give it to the tax men. It will be enough for both of us."

Why does Peter respond to the tax men the way he does? In what sense is this an attempt by Peter to save face?

3. How do you interpret the lesson Jesus is teaching Peter here? How does it relate to our escape from Me-Ville?

Whether we're judging ourselves against the practices of others or judging others by how we operate, we are displacing Jesus from the center and replacing him with someone or something that can't bear the weight and hasn't earned the spot. . . . Despite our conscious and unconscious attempts to put ourselves, or occasionally other people, in the center, Jesus confronts us with the reality that he has never given the center up, and he displaces us all over again.

4. Why might we need to be continually delivered from Me-Ville by Jesus?

5. What does it say about the human condition that even religious devotion can be tainted by self-absorption?

6. What does it say about God that he anticipates and accommodates that tendency?

7. Where might God be reminding you these days that not you but Christ is the center?

8: THE BLESSINGS OF DISCOMFORT

FROM CHAPTER FOUR: JESUS DELIVERS US

Because we've inherited not only the scripts of our religion but also the scripts of our culture, we look for ways of distinguishing ourselves from one another, of being "holier than thou" or "more relevant than thee"—whatever we're more capable of pulling off.

1. Think of the phrase "good Christian" and describe the person who comes to mind. What does the person do habitually? What does the person categorically refuse to do? What books are on the person's nightstand? How does the person talk? Dress?

2. How closely do you resemble the person you described? How did you come to think of these notions as being what makes a Christian "good"?

3. Read the Beatitudes from Matthew 5:3–12.

    You're blessed when you're at the end of your rope. With less of you there is more of God and his rule.
    You're blessed when you feel you've lost what is most dear to you. Only then can you be embraced by the One most dear to you.
    You're blessed when you're content with just who you

are—no more, no less. That's the moment you find yourselves proud owners of everything that can't be bought.

You're blessed when you've worked up a good appetite
for God. He's food and drink in the best meal you'll ever eat.

You're blessed when you care. At the moment of being
"care-full," you find yourselves cared for.

You're blessed when you get your inside world—your
mind and heart—put right. Then you can see God in the
outside world.

You're blessed when you can show people how to cooper-
ate instead of compete or fight. That's when you discover
who you really are, and your place in God's family.

You're blessed when your commitment to God provokes
persecution. The persecution drives you even deeper into
God's kingdom.

Not only that—count yourselves blessed every time people put you down or throw you out or speak lies about you to
discredit me. What it means is that the truth is too close for
comfort and they are uncomfortable. You can be glad when
that happens—give a cheer, even!—for though they don't like
it, I do! And all heaven applauds. And know that you are in
good company. My prophets and witnesses have always gotten into this kind of trouble.

4. Which of these "beatitudes" describes something you're going
   through lately?

5. In what ways are these beatitudes a kind of "press against" (what the author calls *agere contra*) the impulses of Me-Ville?

6. In what ways does a list like this tempt people to compare themselves to others? How can we guard ourselves from that temptation?

7. What help has God made available to you in pressing against the temptations of Me-Ville and your escape from it? How are you taking advantage of that help these days?

9: SO MANY SETS OF FOOTPRINTS IN THE SAND

FROM CHAPTER FIVE: JESUS BINDS US TOGETHER

We realize soon enough upon our departure from Me-Ville that more than one set of footprints track through the sand; Jesus is not plucking us individually out of trouble but gathering together a people for himself, establishing a kingdom that will reign forever, and teaching us how to inhabit that kingdom as a community of faith.... Regardless of how you and I feel about each other, we are being bound together by Jesus.

1. How involved in a church have you been over the course of your life?

2. In what ways is your relationship with the Christian church similar to your relationship with God? In what ways are they different?

3. The church is, generally, in decline in most countries in the Western world. Why do you think that is that so? Why are some Christians tempted to abandon the church? Why are some non-Christians unwilling to give church a shot?

The danger of invidious comparison, the threat to our spiritual well-being ... comes when we shove Jesus out of the center in order to get a better look at our friends, relatives, and, above all, rivals—to size them up, to ascertain what they have that we don't and what we have that they don't.

To thus shove Jesus from his rightful place in relation to us is to dis-integrate
what God has brought together; the logical conclusion of this kind of dis-inte-
gration is a more deeply entrenched sense of superbia than we earlier escaped.

4. How does invidious comparison of ourselves to other people get
   in the way of our relationship with God?

5. Read Luke 11:24–26.

When a corrupting spirit is expelled from someone, it
drifts along through the desert looking for an oasis, some
unsuspecting soul it can bedevil. When it doesn't find anyone, it says, "I'll go back to my old haunt." On return, it
finds the person swept and dusted, but vacant. It then runs
out and rounds up seven other spirits dirtier than itself and
they all move in, whooping it up. That person ends up far
worse than if he'd never gotten cleaned up in the first place.

In what ways might a relationship with God that doesn't
involve other Christians be considered "vacant"? In what
ways is such a person vulnerable in his or her faith?

6. How does being part of a church help us in our journey out of
   Me-Ville?

7. How could the regular practice of confession with people you
   trust enhance your relationship with God? Your relationship with
   the church?

10 IF GOD SAYS IT'S OKAY

FROM CHAPTER SIX: GETTING IN THE WAY OF JESUS

Getting in the way of Jesus reminds us of our finiteness but immediately thereafter reminds us that we've now been called beyond that, that out of love for us God is leading us to a new and better place. The best we can do for ourselves and those around us and, really, the whole world is to say, "He leads the way. Follow him."

1. Talk about a time you've been confronted by your own limitations—at work, maybe, or in some social setting. What happened? What did it do to your mood? Your motivations?

2. What does it mean to be "called beyond" our limitations? What's intimidating about that? What's encouraging?

3. What role does faith play in following God "to a new and better place"? What role does obedience play?

The farther Jesus leads us from Me-Ville to the place he has prepared for us, the less sensible it is to go back, and the less fulfilling each visit will be. … When you notice Jesus, especially where you weren't expecting to see him, you notice that what he's doing and saying are a lot more interesting, a lot more creative than what you're doing and saying.

4. Read Acts 11:5–18.

"Recently I was in the town of Joppa praying. I fell into a
trance and saw a vision: Something like a huge blanket, low-
ered by ropes at its four corners, came down out of heaven
and settled on the ground in front of me. Milling around on
the blanket were farm animals, wild animals, reptiles, birds—
you name it, it was there. Fascinated, I took it all in.

"Then I heard a voice: 'Go to it, Peter—kill and eat.' I
said, 'Oh, no, Master. I've never so much as tasted food that
wasn't kosher.' The voice spoke again: 'If God says it's okay,
it's okay.' This happened three times, and then the blanket
was pulled back up into the sky.

"Just then three men showed up at the house where I was
staying, sent from Caesarea to get me. The Spirit told me to
go with them, no questions asked. So I went with them, I
and six friends, to the man who had sent for me. He told us
how he had seen an angel right in his own house, real as his
next-door neighbor, saying, 'Send to Joppa and get Simon,
the one they call Peter. He'll tell you something that will save
your life—in fact, you and everyone you care for.'

"So I started in, talking. Before I'd spoken half a dozen
sentences, the Holy Spirit fell on them just as he did on us
the first time. I remembered Jesus' words: 'John baptized
with water; you will be baptized with the Holy Spirit.' So I
ask you: If God gave the same exact gift to them as to us
when we believed in the Master Jesus Christ, how could I
object to God?"

Hearing it all laid out like that, they quieted down. And

then, as it sank in, they started praising God. "It's really hap-pened! God has broken through to the other nations, opened them up to Life!"

What prepared Peter for this experience?

5. Why do you suppose Peter had the same vision, the same con-versation, three times?

6. When is it appropriate to ask questions about what God is telling you to do? When is it appropriate to simply obey? How can we tell the difference?

7. How can we help each other to figure out what Jesus is telling us and to obey what he's commanding us?

11 OUR COVENANT FRIEND

FROM THE AFTERWORD TO *DELIVER US FROM ME-VILLE*

God loves the foolish as much as he loves the wise, so we might as well admit when we've been foolish and enjoy a good laugh about it every now and then.

1. Think back to a time when you made a wild promise to God. What prompted you to do it?

2. Whatever came of that promise?

3. Read Matthew 6:7–13 (NIV).

When you pray, do not keep on babbling like pagans, for they think they will be heard because of their many words. Do not be like them, for your Father knows what you need before you ask him.

"This, then, is how you should pray:
"'Our Father in heaven,
hallowed be your name,
your kingdom come,
your will be done
on earth as it is in heaven.

Give us today our daily bread.

Forgive us our debts,

   as we also have forgiven our debtors.

And lead us not into temptation,

   but deliver us from the evil one.'"

In what sense is this a bold prayer? In what sense is it easy to pray?

4. The author divides this prayer into two parts. Is this a sensible division? How would you characterize the difference between the author's part one and part two?

5. Try to summarize the Lord's Prayer into one sentence or one phrase. Talk about the challenges in coming up with your summary.

God didn't come all the way from his kingdom to Me-Ville to get me simply to part ways with me; God wants me—and with me, you and really all of us—to be in his kingdom, which is where he is, which as the Lord's Prayer suggests, is on earth even as it is in heaven.

6. Having worked your way through *Deliver Us from Me-Ville*, how do you see yourself relating differently to God? To the world around you?

7. What are some practical ways you can keep God's kingdom in view as you go through your day-to-day life?

A hip and humorous journalistic approach to finding your place in God's big picture.

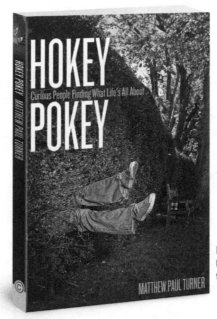

Hokey Pokey
Matthew Paul Turner
978-0-7814-4536-8

Popular author Matthew Paul Turner explores the universal desire to live with purpose. Packing his hipster humor and irreverent sensibilities, Matthew takes to the road to collect uncommon wisdom from people who are living out their callings—from pastors, to professors, to the guy next door. Each conversation offers personal insights for finding your place in God's big picture, and young adults will be encouraged and challenged in their pursuit of a life well lived.

God is love.
crazy, relentless, all-powerful love.

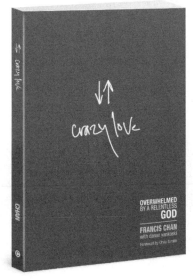

Crazy Love
Francis Chan
978-1-4347-6851-3
francischan.org

Think about it. God, the creator of everything—from nitrogen to pine needles; from oceans to E-minor—THAT God, loves you. And after we rebelled and rejected Him, He loved us so much that He made a plan to rescue us so we might be with him forever. So yeah, that's a little crazy. But it's true and it's the good news that has changed billions of lives over the past two thousand years.

Once you encounter God's love as Francis describes it, you cannot go back to a life of simples do's and don'ts. God doesn't want your begrudging leftovers or even your good intentions. He wants you—heart, soul, and mind. That's why you are here. That's why we're all here. Don't miss it.

Get yours today at DavidCCook.com or a Christian retailer near you.